Who do You Think They Were?

The Memorials of Ripon Cathedral

Contributors

Research and Text: Derek Ching, Andrew Coulson, Ian Curteis, Frances Demain, Susan Ford, Toria Forsyth-Moser, Kirsty Hallett, David Lee, David Murfet, Moira Stalker, John Wimpress

Design: Ian Stalker

Photos: Ian Stalker unless otherwise attributed

Drawings: Eileen Walters unless otherwise attributed

Index: David Lee

Editor: Toria Forsyth-Moser

Acknowledgements

The Heritage Lottery Fund
This book is the outcome of research undertaken as part of "Your Passport to Ripon Cathedral's Heritage", a project funded by the Heritage Lottery Fund. We would like to express our gratitude to the Heritage Lottery Fund for making possible not only this book, but a large programme of events and activities at Ripon Cathedral.

Other information and advice
Our gratitude goes to: Diana Balmforth, Joy Calvert, Dean Chapman, May & Howard Clarke, Geoffrey Collin, Brian Crosse, Anne Ford, Bill Forster, Cathy Hellier, Joan Kirby, Priestley Kirby, Barbara Oakes, Frances & Richard Redpath, Dorothy & Maurice Taylor and many others.

Kind permission to reproduce pictures was given by:
bephotographed.co.uk, Colonial Williamsburg Foundation, Bill Emmerson, Rachael Fox-Evans, Royal Fusiliers Association, Imperial War Museum, Ingleby Jefferson, Newby Hall, Southold Historical Society, Virginia Historical Society, West Yorkshire Archive Service.

Faces on front cover (clockwise from top right)
William Weddell, Lt. R.N. Jefferson (*courtesy Mr Ingleby Jefferson*), Dorothy Oxley, Katharine Kinnear *(courtesy of The Imperial War Museum)*, Hugh Ripley.

Contents

	Page
Preface	4
Introduction	5
Memorials: Styles and Materials	7
Epitaphs and Symbols	13
Women and Children	20
Medieval Tombs	27
Memorials to Clergymen	38
17th Century	44
The Great and the Sometimes Not So Good	52
Memorials with an American Connection	68
Ripon and the British Empire	75
World War I Memorials and the Reredos	86
The Display of Heraldry	95
The Graveyard	110
Index	120

Preface

Those who visit Ripon Cathedral do so for a variety of reasons. Since Wilfrid first established his 'Mission Church' people have, for example, come here to pray and to draw close to God in both joy and need. Others have come to seek counsel and still more have come to see beauty and encounter holiness. Today people come in just the same way, not only contributing to an ongoing living tradition but also underlying the existence of Ripon Cathedral as both house of prayer and major visitor centre.

At our Cathedral, you will find a wealth of 'treasures' wrapped up in the offering of woodworkers, stonemasons, silversmiths and other craftspeople who have given of their best down the centuries. Of these treasures there are our memorials, the subject of this book, which themselves not only demonstrate the finest ability of people to create an object of lasting beauty and worth but also tell us so much of the history of those who have been associated with the Cathedral since its very beginnings.

The fact is that for centuries families have used memorials to remember their loved ones by and to mark significant achievement and benefaction. This book will draw you into a world of discovery and will entice you not only to learn of the history of our Cathedral but also, through a systematic appreciation of the monuments featured, will engage you into the very life and times of the people who are commemorated.

My thanks are due to all those who through their research and generosity have made this book possible and particularly to Toria Forsyth-Moser and the Heritage Lottery Fund.

Let the discovery begin and as you walk through the Cathedral may you sense God's blessing for your own lives.

The Very Rev'd Keith Jukes
Dean of Ripon

Introduction

Walking around Ripon Cathedral you cannot fail to notice the evocative memorials, commemorating forebears, lining the walls of the nave aisles. Each memorial has its own story to reveal. You might ask yourself, "Who were these people, what did they do, why did they die?" Perhaps you might want to learn a bit more about these memorials: what they can teach us about heraldry, design and the changing use of materials? Maybe you are interested in Latin and the poetry of epitaphs, the use of symbols in a Christian context or even social history.

Looking at and studying memorials can be a rich and rewarding experience. The men, women and children commemorated on these monuments are representatives of past generations, of the people who helped to shape the society in which we live. The study of memorials can help us to connect to our roots by enabling us to understand the contributions of those who have gone before.

Funerary monuments, however, are not only a valuable historical source, but also give meaning to the loss we suffer when a loved one dies; or give expression to the grief of a whole community during wars and plagues. The reredos in Ripon Cathedral, for example, is an evocative monument to collective remembering. The statue of the risen beardless Christ portrayed at the same young age as many of the soldiers who die in wars, reflects the Christian belief that death is only the beginning of new life.

Gazing at many of the memorials, we are reminded that people throughout the centuries dealt with the sorts of issues and questions with which we too struggle. They help us to connect to the past, to meditate on the frailty of human life, to question the existence of an after-life or to trace our individual roots by doing family history research.

Memorials tell us about the past – what people believed, what trades and occupations they held, their taste (sometimes garish or overly sentimental), or even their sense of humour, social attitudes, fashion.

Should only the deserving be remembered? Those men and women who made such unselfish contributions that we feel they are worthy of a memorial in a special place? What about the poor who have been forgotten because their families could not afford to pay for a stone tablet? Or those who could not trust others to show the required appreciation for their achievements and erected their own memorials and even composed the epitaph to show the world what worthy lives they had lived?

Some are remembered because they were loved and valued, others because their families had influence and wealth. Funerary monuments have been status symbols for thousands of years. It was the Roman statesman Cato the Elder who said, "After I'm dead I'd rather have people ask why I have no monument than why I have one."

Memorials can tell us about the history of religion, and even of differing practices of Christianity throughout the centuries. Several monuments in Ripon Cathedral, for example, were vandalized during the Civil War, in the middle of the 17th century, by soldiers following a more Protestant tradition of simplicity in church architecture and decoration.

Some memorials can speak to the heart. Who is not moved by the eloquence of the broken snowdrop on Henry William Strickland's memorial; the little boy who died much too young?

Above all, memorials are signposts. They remind us of our own mortality and lead us to think of the things for which we would like to be remembered.

Toria Forsyth-Moser

A dedicated group of Cathedral volunteers has researched the memorials of Ripon Cathedral and compiled and illustrated this book as part of a Heritage Lottery funded project. Whilst addressing various aspects, we have only been able to highlight a sample of the memorials in the Cathedral and its graveyard. For every interesting memorial or person included in the book, there is at least one who has been left out. It is hoped that our aim - to produce an overall picture, to share with you a reflection of the rich heritage of people associated with and commemorated in Ripon Cathedral - has nevertheless been achieved.

Note from the editor: Unless indicated otherwise, all epitaph transcriptions are transcribed from the Ripon Cathedral Inventory (editor Diana Balmforth). Errors and oddities are commonly found on inscriptions, and are not usually pointed out specifically. The sources at the end of each article are a guide to further reading or research; they are not meant to be exhaustive.

Memorials: Styles and Materials

Before the Reformation (1534) not many memorials were to be seen in Ripon Minster (Ripon Minster only became a Cathedral in 1836; the first to be created since the Reformation). Its walls were covered in colour, often with frescoes, of which some remain in the south transept. Wealthy families were commemorated in stone table tombs with effigies, such as the Markenfield tombs in the north transept, carved in local limestone, placed in chapels which became the family burial place. Others who contributed to the building have their heraldic devices carved in stone, both in the nave and in the choir.

After the Reformation, when the Minster became a parish church, burial slabs of stone appear in the floor, while important individuals and families were commemorated in wall monuments of stone, such as those of **Moses Fowler** (1608) in the south choir aisle (Chapel of the Holy Spirit) and Sir **Edward Blackett** (1718). The latter has migrated to the south west tower from the north transept where it originally stood more prominently. These two monuments show the transition from a recumbent effigy, with members of the family kneeling in prayer (common at the beginning of the seventeenth century), to a semi-recumbent figure, with a magnificent wig, flanked by two standing figures, more realistic in portraiture, over a hundred years later. Each is placed in an architectural setting typical of its period – late Elizabethan and High Baroque. There is an interesting third memorial, in the

Memorials in stone: Fowler (above) and Blackett (below)

7

nave, also of a common type of its period: the kneeling bust portrait of **Hugh Ripley,** last Wakeman and first Mayor of Ripon (1637). Unfortunately, this was

defaced in the Civil War (1642 – 1646) and not re-erected until 1730. Another example of the bust effigy can be found in the Library, that of Dean **Higgin** (1624). Like that of Hugh Ripley, it was badly damaged, but not restored.

The finest stone memorial in the Cathedral is undoubtedly that of **William Weddell** (1789). Weddell was a prominent collector of sculpture on the Grand Tour and also a patron of the architect Robert Adam. His memorial, by the noted 18th century sculptor Nollekens, has a fine portrait bust on a pedestal, framed by a rotunda, (like those in the gardens of his home, Newby Hall), based on the Choragic Monument of Lysicrates in Athens: a fitting tribute to his interests and status.

The last Wakeman
Hugh Ripley

The stone used in most of these memorials is magnesian limestone or sandstone, both quarried nearby or elsewhere in Yorkshire. The earlier effigies were coloured, but little of this colour now exists. With the eighteenth and early nineteenth century there came a change to a more popular material – white marble, sometimes backed with dark or grey marble for contrast. A fine example of these can be found in the group of memorials to the **Mallorie** and **Aislabie** families, buried in the eastern chapels of the south transept and now in its gallery. The best and earliest of these is that of Sir **John Mallorie** (1666); those of his descendants have more modest wall plaques. The walls of the Cathedral aisles and transepts carry an increasing number of smaller, more modest memorials and these, as did those of the earlier period, reflect the architectural styles then fashionable. Baroque gave way to classical: the cartouche, or inscription contained in a round frame, sometimes carved in imitation of cloth, or curves derived from this, gave way to angular memorial plaques, as the neo-classical style took over. The Gothic revival style never had the same impact here at Ripon: there is an example behind the font in the south nave aisle (**John and Isabella Elliott** and their children).

William Weddell memorial
by Nollekens

Typical of the neo-classical style, which became very popular, is the memorial based on the Greek stele or column, whose shape and simple pediment is given to flat panels with their long inscriptions. A notable example of this can be found in the north choir aisle (St Peter's Chapel). It records the fate of the children of **James Webber,** Dean from 1828 to 1847. Most died young, nearly all of them tragically, including cot death, drowning in the Thames and being run over by a steam engine! Their Latin inscription includes a moving Italian quotation from Tasso.

Webber memorial

Oxley memorial

At the end of the nineteenth century there was a slight variation in the type of stone. We find memorials in alabaster in the north transept and in the south-west tower; the latter an eccentric memorial to the **Oxley** family. From this time, perhaps due to increasing lack of space, memorials become smaller and confined to incised inscriptions, sometimes with touches of heraldry.

Wood is a far more perishable medium for memorials, as history has shown, but there is one magnificent example in this Cathedral: the Reredos and High Altar, designed and executed by Sir Ninian Comper in 1923, in the high Gothic style. The splendour of its gilt and coloured figures is a stark contrast to the plain arcading on either side which bears the incised names of the majority of those from Ripon who fell in the First World War, whose memorial this is. The figures themselves are of stone, with alabaster heads and hands, sculpted by William D. Gough, who did much work of this nature for Comper. In the nave, by way of contrast, there is a combination of marble, wood, copper and silver in the lively Arts and Crafts style pulpit carried out by Henry Wilson in 1913, incorporating the name of the donor by way of memorial.

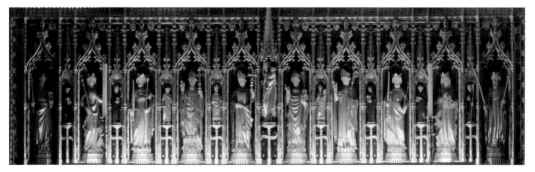

Detail of reredos by Sir Ninian Comper (1923)

Wood and metal have once more come into their own as memorials in the form of modern furnishing. These include the screen and pyx of the Holy Spirit Chapel by Leslie Durbin (1970), the nave altar, chairs and choir stalls by Illingworth and Partridge (1989), and the series of statues of a mother and child by Harold Gosney (1998 - 2000).

The Pieta: one of three bronze sculptures by Harold Gosney

In the Middle Ages glass often became a form of memorial, its panels often incorporating the heraldic shields of the donors, as can be seen at York Minster. Ripon, however, suffered terribly in the desecration of the Civil War in 1643 and all that remains of its medieval glass can be found at the west end of the south nave aisle, mounted in sixteen panels against plain glass in 1950. There is another collection of heraldic painted glass from a later period, displaced by the great restorations of the nineteenth century, now placed in the east window of the library. It includes work by the notable York glazier, William Peckitt.

The restorations undertaken between 1828 and 1900 saw the use of glass, painted and stained, come into its own again as a form of memorial. Just as the number of wall memorials proliferated, so did new glass windows, whose biblical subjects now included inscriptions commemorating the donors, often with their coats of arms.

Their names are mainly those of notable families in the neighbourhood and dignitaries of the new diocese, to whose foundation the great east window was re-glazed as a memorial, first in 1854 by Wailes and then remodelled on enlargement (1894) by Hemming: it shows the contrasting growth of range and delicacy of colours.

Ripon Cathedral's only Medieval glass

At the east end of the north nave aisle are three windows which illustrate the great change in techniques and styles. The earliest is the **Grantley** memorial window, painted by Thomas Willement in 1840. It traces the descent of the Norton family, Baron Grantley of Markenfield, from John of Gaunt, and includes in the central coat of arms the quartering of the 'stars and stripes' of the Washington family. This window is also interesting in that, alone among its fellows, it has no reference to any biblical or religious subject.

To the right is a smaller window reverting to the medieval custom of a biblical subject accompanied by a smaller kneeling figure of the donor or, in this case, subject of the memorial. Here it is Bishop **Boyd Carpenter** (1912), a celebrated preacher in his day, which may account for the subject of St Paul's preaching. The bishop was also interested in boxing; perhaps this accounts for the appearance of several pugilistic types in the crowd! The window is a fine example of the work of Sir Ninian Comper, who also designed the reredos.

The third window, to the left reflects a recent development in the treatment of glass in Cathedrals. As in the south nave aisle fragments of medieval and later glass have been gathered together, this time mounted as a band across clear glass. What distinguishes this window is the inclusion of engraved plain glass: a quotation from the poetry of Dean **Le Grice**, whose memorial it forms.

Modern glass is the most striking memorial form in the Cathedral. The **Sykes** memorial window in the north transept, by Harry Harvey in 1977, shows scenes from the life of

The St Wilfrid window (1977)

Detail from the Dean Le Grice window

Christic the Judge (2006): a modern
Glass memorial

St Wilfrid, to whom this chapel is now dedicated. Harvey uses fragmented heads and subjects together with touches of clear glass which give this decidedly modern window a medieval feel. A more traditional approach, but with a sparing use of colour against clear glass can be found in the **Crabtree** memorial window in the south transept gallery, by Warren Wilson (1957).

Last, but by no means least, is the most innovative window, designed by John Lawson, the chief designer for Goddard & Gibbs of London: a glass panel of Christ the Judge, whose figure, in Romanesque style, appears to be hung free of the wall within the arch separating the north-west tower from the north nave aisle, above the new Chapel of Justice and Peace, which replaces the old Consistory Court. This gives an unusual perspective and dimension to a traditional form and was given as a memorial (2006) to **Jean Emmerson**.

David Murfet

Notes and Sources:

We thank Mr Bill Emmerson for information regarding the glass panel in the Chapel of Justice and Peace. The designer John Lawson came out of retirement especially to design this work.

FORSTER – ROBSON – DEADMAN: *Ripon Cathedral: Its History and Architecture*, (1993)

Epitaphs and Symbols

Epitaphs: Prepare to Follow Me!

The earliest transcript from a memorial stone in the graveyard is that for the **Allanson** family of Sharow:

> Near this place was buried Richd. Allanson of Sharow 3rd October, 1625, æ. 81; George his son 13th Feby. 1671, æ. 87; Stephen his son 9th July, 1677, æ. 50; John Allanson, the son of Stephen, 20th April, 1724, æ. 60; Ann his wife 23rd Augt., 1738, æ. 69, who had 19 children; Mr. George Allanson, Supervisor, their seventh son, 11th Feb., 1756, æ. 55; Mr. Michael Allanson, son of Michael Allanson, Attorney at law, 29th Sept., 1733, æ. 27.

Richard Allanson was born in 1541 and it was his grandson, Stephen who fathered the nineteen children referred to in the inscription. Although this appears a large family, one stone commemorates a far greater number of descendants:

> Here lieth the body of **Margaret Lupton,** late wife of Mr. Sampson Lupton of Braisty Woods, in Netherdale, who departed this life the 2nd of November, anno Domini 1718, in the 74th year of her age, and lived to be mother and grandmother to above 150 children, and at the baptizing of the first grandchild, the child had ten grandfathers and grandmothers then present.

With "above 150" children and grandchildren to her credit, the only puzzling item is how one child comes to have "ten grandfathers and grandmothers"!

The graveyard inscription of **William Milburn**, who died aged 78 on 31st January 1752, taken from the headstone in the graveyard of Ripon Cathedral, reads:

> Remember man as thou goes by,
> As thou art now, so once was I,
> As l am now, so thou must be,
> Therefore prepare to follow me.

While this may appear a somewhat stern reminder to the mourner/visitor, the moralistic style of the message is typical of many graves in many Churchyards in this country. Death is an event which is inevitable and should you fail to think about your own mortality, there are many examples of a "warning from the grave".

The range of emotions and observations carried by Ripon's epitaphs is, however, as diverse as the population of this ancient city.

The role of the epitaph

In present times the message placed on a headstone is usually a mix of dates, relationships and a brief quotation, usually (but not always) from a religious text. From the first known inscriptions on graves, there was also the chance to make a public statement of grief, of the exemplary character of the deceased, or of your trust in a better place in your next life.

Amongst the most poignant are possibly those found on children's graves:

> Happy the babe, who privileg'd by fate
> To shorter labour and a lighter weight,
> Receiv'd but yesterday the gift of breath,
> Order'd to-morrow to return to death.
>
> (**John Wilson**, 14 months)

> He tasted of life's bitter cup,
> Refus'd to drink the portion up,
> Then turn'd his little head aside,
> Disgusted with the taste and died.
>
> (**Thomas Harper**, 3 years)

> Rest happy babes in heaven above,
> On earth short was your stay,
> Because the Lord your souls did love,
> He soon took you away.
>
> (**Mary**, 2 years & **Hannah March**, 8 years)

> Short was his race, the longer is his rest,
> God called him hence, because he thought it best,
> And now he's gone such is the good report,
> He liv'd and dy'd belov'd of every sort.
>
> (**Joseph Grayson**, 17 years)

Some mourners seemed however to take the opportunity to make a public, if somewhat belated, apology to their nearest and dearest:

> To thee, O venerable shade,
> Who long hast in oblivion laid,
> This stone I here erect;
> A tribute small for what thou'st done,
> Deign to accept this small return,
> Pardon the long neglect.
> To thy long labours, to thy care,
> Thy son, who lives thy present heir,
> This grateful tribute owe.
> Spirit divine ! what thanks are due,
> This will thy memory renew,
> It's all I can bestow.

(Erected by the son of **Francis Iles**, died 17th February, 1794, aged 87)

And still others wrote a 'reference' for their servants:

> In manners plain, in worth approv'd,
> A friend sincere, a servant lov'd,
> Little in wealth, in bounty great,
> Narrow the means, the will compleat,
> Who saw no strife without his grief,
> No want, but gave or wished relief,
> Large mind restrain'd by low degree,
> A labourer for charity.
> The good rewarding all his pains,
> He that was this was Charles Haynes.

(**Charles Haynes** was park-keeper to the Hon John Aislabie of Studley)

From 1728, a brief but descriptive account:

> Here Henry Raper
> Lies in dust,
> His stature small,
> His mind was just.

Many more were examples of family grief:

> The widow though mourning her partner's demise;
> The mother though grieving the loss of her son;
> Yet rememb'ring that He who took them is wise,
> Submissively crieth "let His will be done".

(From a young widow who had buried her husband aged 28 and her son in 1827)

Some warned us:

> Ye young rely not on to-morrow's dawn,
> No certain tenure is allotted man;
> On Tuesday morn I trod the verdant lawn,
> On Friday measured out my narrow span.

(Grave of the **Terry** brothers aged 18 months and 9 years)

But some were still optimistic:

> Yet death may choose his keenest dart,
> And give the grave its clod;
> It only frees the better part,
> And sends it home to God.

(**John Dowson,** 30th April, 1777, aged 68)

> Dear friends for me don't morn & weep,
> For in the dust I soundly sleep;
> A troubled world I've left behind,
> Eternal glory for to find.

(**Fanny Cock,** 30th May, 1840, aged 23)

The opportunity to make a point, knowing full well that you would never be accountable for any consequence, is seen in the case of a long suffering patient who still has concerns over his medical care:

> Afflictions sore long time I bore,
> Physicians were in vain,
> Till God did please
> My life with death to ease,
> And free me from my pain.

(**Thomas Bell,** who died 1st July, 1807, aged 34)

A pale consumption gave the fatal blow,
The stroke was certain. tho' the effect was slow;
With lingering pain God saw me sore oppress't,
Pitied my signs and kindly gave me rest.

(**John Chapman**, died 27th October 1839, aged 23)

Still others just wanted to let you know that they really had been ill:

I told the Lord my sore distress,
With heavy groans and tears;
He gave my sharpest torments ease,
And silenced all my fears.

(**Catherine Nelson**, died 20th February, 1819, aged 29)

And then there is the chance to metaphorically "stick out your tongue":

Adieu! vain world, enough I've had of thee,
I value not what thou canst say of me,
Thy smiles I court not, nor thy frowns I fear,
'Tis all as one to me, my head lies quiet here.

(**Charles Davis**, date unclear)

More warnings offered to us by those who have gone before:
Ye living men survey the tomb
Where you must quickly dwell
Hark! how the awful summons sounds
In every funeral knel.

(**John Anderson,** died 25th January, 1838, aged 77)

...and finally an epitaph, that despite taking good taste to its very limit, has been a favourite with many:

Here lies poor, but honest, Bryan Tunstall,
he was a most expert angler,
until death envious of his merit, threw out his line,
hook'd him, and landed him here
the 21st day of April 1790.

Andrew Coulson

Notes and Sources

The text for the epitaphs in this section was taken from:

WILSON, T.: "*A verbatim copy of all the monuments, gravestones and other sepulchral memorials in Ripon Cathedral and its burial ground.*" (1847)

For those interested in epitaphs see: WRIGHT, Geoffrey N.: *Discovering Epitaphs,* (2004)

Symbols

Symbolism is a language deployed by artists since the beginning of time. So many human emotions and attitudes often cannot be adequately expressed in words; grief and the fear of dying feature prominently among these.

Any examination of gravestones and memorials must therefore include some consideration of the symbols used. We can admire the skill of the stonemason in producing some wonderful designs, but they merit further study as the symbols used all have a meaning. These can refer to the spiritual aspirations of the deceased, his or her occupation, family history and so on.

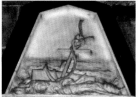

Coffin and anchor: death at sea

Symbols can have more than one meaning. For example an anchor generally symbolises hope and security and someone at rest, but it is also used to indicate a naval profession such as the anchor on the memorial to **Robert Darley Waddilove.** His tablet depicts a coffin floating in the waves with an anchor. If people were buried at sea it was in a shroud, not a coffin, so in this context, the anchor tied to a coffin symbolises his death whilst serving in the navy and perhaps his having found security and rest in the afterlife.

Broken snowdrop: death in childhood

Detail from Bowman memorial

Flowers are a symbol of life and death and are often used for young people. A good example of this is the memorial to **Henry Strickland**, which has a lovely design of snowdrops. It is appropriately poignant as one snowdrop has a broken stem and has fallen to the ground.

The memorial to **Thomas More Bowman** has a design of a bow, which is obviously a play on his name. There is also a staff with a serpent curled around it. He was a surgeon and this is the symbol of *Aesculapius,* the famous healer of Greek mythology.

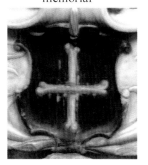

Crossed bones: is this a pun on the family name?

Skulls and bones are obviously associated with death, but on the **Hellen Bayne** memorial there are crossed bones derived from the Bayne family coat of arms. Bayne/Bone - a play on the family name.

Urns are often seen on memorials and are worth a closer look, as there are two different types. An empty and draped urn represents death while an urn with a flame is symbolic of new life. The memorial wall to **Christopher Oxley**, for instance, depicts a draped funerary urn with acanthus decoration. This plant is one of the earliest cemetery motifs, popular already in ancient Greek architecture as the acanthus is associated with rocky ground, where Greek cemeteries were usually located. In Christianity the acanthus represents the heavenly garden.

It is not unusual to see workmen's tools, as these would indicate the deceased's trade or profession. For example, a mallet and chisel would be used for a joiner and hammer and pincers for a smith. What is unusual is to see workmen's tools on a female's memorial and these are evident on the tablet to **Elizabeth Garnett,** known affectionately as the "navvies friend" (*see chapter on Women and Children*).

The very fine bust, which is the **Weddell** memorial, has a serpent on it. While the serpent is usually a symbol of evil, this one has its tail in its mouth, and as such represents eternity.

Workmen's tools: the memorial to the "navvies friend"

When studying memorials in Ripon Cathedral, look for books, cherubs, flowers, and anything unusual, as well as the cross with which we are all familiar. It will become an interesting study.

Susan Ford

Notes and Sources

For further reading on Christian symbols see ELLWOOD POST, W.: *Saints, Signs, and Symbols* (1964 and following editions)

FERGUSON, George: *Signs & Symbols in Christian Art* (1954 and following editions)

Eternity represented by a serpent with its tail in its mouth

Women and Children

The majority of the memorials in the Cathedral are dedicated to men; women generally only feature as wives, mothers or daughters. Women are celebrated for what are seen as typically female qualities: obedience, faithfulness, humility, piety, affection. How different from the way most women of the 21st century would wish to be remembered! Look for example at **Elizabeth Clark** (wall north transept), who died in 1809 and who is remembered as a figure of "domestic virtue", being a "faithful wife and affectionate mother of ten children". **Deborah Metcalfe** (wall south transept) was a "dutiful and affectionate wife who bore a long and painful illness with great patience and Christian fortitude".

One of the earlier memorials, that of **Hellen Bayne** (south aisle wall) is remarkable for the date of her death, which is transcribed as 1694/5, a reference to the old Julian calendar which, until 1752, celebrated March 25th as New Year's Day. Hellen's memorial is a grained marble cartouche (a stone representation of a scroll) with an urn above, which represents death; swathes of acanthus leaves, one of the oldest cemetery motifs, symbolising the heavenly garden; and mourning drapes.

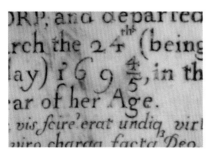

Detail from Hellen Bayne memorial: the apparently uncertain year of death is due to the use of the Julian Calendar.

Hellen is described as "a truly affectionate and most deservedly beloved wife". She bore nine children and was only 33 when she died. There follows a Latin inscription, which is said to have been composed by Christopher Wyvil, Dean of Ripon. Part of the translation reads: "Let womankind repair to this monument, that from thence they may learn the duty of a wife and the tenderness of a mother. Do not enquire whether it was erected in memory of her piety or the grief of her spouse. Her death was the occasion of its being placed here".

Childbirth was fraught with danger and there are several poignant memorials to women who died following childbirth. **Faith Northcliffe** (floor north aisle) died on June 17th 1733, aged 26, having given birth to her only son, **Fairfax Northcliffe,** on June 5th. He died five weeks later on July 16th. Their memorial is a grey slate flagstone and is an excellent example of work from this period.

Juliana Braithwaite (floor south aisle) the wife of Christopher Braithwaite, died in 1769 aged 35 having had two children.. Her husband then took a second wife, this time Elizabeth Braithwaite the daughter of Edmund Braithwaite, by whom he had two children, Christopher and Elizabeth, who both died in infancy. Elizabeth herself died in 1773 aged 33. Their memorial is a slate flagstone in good condition.

Isabella Stevenson (wall south aisle) died in 1825 aged 31 and John her son died in infancy.

In stark contrast with these early deaths, two spinster sisters, **Sarah and Harriet Clough**, (wall south aisle) died at the great ages of 95 and 99 respectively. Their wall tablet is of polished white marble, mounted on a polished black slate slab. Their Latin inscription translates as "Virtue lives after death".

A married lady, who lived to 93, but who does not appear to have borne any children, was **Jane Featherstone** (nave wall north tower). Her memorial is a white marble tablet on a black polished slate tablet with acanthus decorations. She is remembered for her "unaffected piety, simplicity of manners and kind consideration for the poor in whose service she was constantly and actively employed … and her many other Christian virtues".

Margaret Chettle (wall north aisle) lived to the age of 81. According to her epitaph, she was "a maiden lady who educated the youth of her sex for forty years at Ripon". She gave her pupils "useful learning and adorned them with her virtues free from the gloss of wealth and ostentation".

Her tribute tells us that she was humble and "her scanty means sprang only from her own industry" which she made to "flow with silent sweetness to help the work of charity".

Her "scanty means" are borne out by her will, which mentions only her best snuff box and two large silver spoons. Nothing else of value is listed and she has only her "best wearing apparel" to leave.

Margaret's nephew, the son of her brother, lived in London; perhaps she came from there as it has not been possible to find any record of her birth or baptism in this area. She was a close friend of the Coates family of Ripon. John Coates, solicitor, erected her memorial and described himself as "her only surviving friend". Dorothy Coates witnessed her will and Mrs Jane Coates, wife of the Rev. John Coates, is the recipient of her "wearing apparel".

Fanny Whitaker (wall south aisle) – a tragic and mysterious tale!

There are several memorials to the Whitaker family but the most interesting one is to Fanny "the beloved and only daughter" of William Whitaker JP, of Breckamore near Ripon (who is commemorated on the same memorial as Fanny, a white marble memorial in the shape of a scroll fixed to a black slate tablet), and the sister of the barrister Mr Marmaduke Whitaker. "Her deeply lamented death resulted from a railway accident at Wilstrop near Green Hammerton" on 16th August 1875. Fanny died the following day. The accident was fully reported at the time in the Ripon Gazette.

Fanny Whitaker's tragic death is commemorated alongside her parents' epitaphs.

Fanny, aged 29, was travelling with two friends from Harrogate to York and as was fitting for young ladies of their position they were in the first class compartment, the last carriage of the train. All went well until the train reached Hammerton, where it reduced speed to cross the River Nidd. After this, there were points to cross and while the first three carriages crossed safely, the three remaining were turned by the points onto the down line. The last carriage was violently overturned and fell onto the edge of the platform. Fanny, who was sitting in the middle facing the engine, was jerked right through the window. The carriage then seemed to right itself, then lurched to the opposite side before finally falling over on the side where Fanny had been thrown. One of her companions climbed out of the window to find Fanny beneath the carriage, unconscious.

Fanny was taken to Wilstrop Hall, but died the next day. Her body was removed to Kirkby Malzeard on the Saturday morning for interment in the family vault. As the cortege passed through Ripon the minute bell of the Cathedral was tolled and several shops were closed out of respect for Fanny and her family.

The burning question was what had caused this terrible accident. An inquest was held and found that the signalman Robert Collinson, though described as an efficient and knowledgeable signalman, had caused the point lever to switch tracks when only half the train had passed, thus causing the last carriage to de-rail. Collinson maintained that the point lever flew over and caught his trousers as he was putting the signal to danger. Whatever the truth of the matter, the foreman of the jury, after only fifteen minutes consultation, returned a verdict of manslaughter on Collinson. Was he made a scapegoat when there was faulty equipment? Was there a cover up? What sentence was Collinson given? The fate of Robert Collinson is still unknown.

Elizabeth Garnett (wall north aisle) - an unsung heroine

This is an unusual memorial for a woman, as it has carved on it traditional workmen's

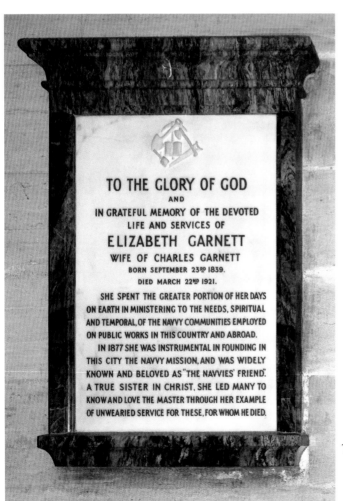

tools: spade, axe, saw, mallet and pickaxe, with an open book in the centre. Elizabeth was known as the Navvies' friend and her tale is an unusual and fascinating one.

She was born in Otley in 1839, the daughter of a vicar and at the age of ten she heard her father preach at the unveiling of a memorial to miners and navvies who had died building Bramhope railway tunnel. This event appears to have made a lasting impact on her later life.

In early middle age, Elizabeth married a parson who died on their honeymoon. She then

The navvy's tools, clearly seen on Elizabeth Garnett's memorial plaque, are sketched at the head of this chapter

TO THE GLORY OF GOD
AND
IN GRATEFUL MEMORY OF THE DEVOTED LIFE AND SERVICES OF
ELIZABETH GARNETT
WIFE OF CHARLES GARNETT
BORN SEPTEMBER 23RD 1839.
DIED MARCH 22ND 1921.
SHE SPENT THE GREATER PORTION OF HER DAYS ON EARTH IN MINISTERING TO THE NEEDS, SPIRITUAL AND TEMPORAL, OF THE NAVVY COMMUNITIES EMPLOYED ON PUBLIC WORKS IN THIS COUNTRY AND ABROAD. IN 1877 SHE WAS INSTRUMENTAL IN FOUNDING IN THIS CITY THE NAVVY MISSION, AND WAS WIDELY KNOWN AND BELOVED AS "THE NAVVIES' FRIEND". A TRUE SISTER IN CHRIST, SHE LED MANY TO KNOW AND LOVE THE MASTER THROUGH HER EXAMPLE OF UNWEARIED SERVICE FOR THESE, FOR WHOM HE DIED.

devoted herself to missionary work visiting the construction workers. A small strong-willed woman, she was appalled by their lives and the danger to their souls.

She had a great affection for them and while she berated and bullied them, she did not look down at them. She called them "mates" and herself a navvy. She formed the Christian Excavators' Union and ran the Quarterly Letter to Navvies for 38 years. In this she campaigned against drink, gave advice on first aid, listed the dead and injured, issued details of jobs etc. It was read widely; in 1904 there were 155,000 copies of one issue. Elizabeth was a remarkable woman who has had little recognition but who had a great influence on the social history of her time.

Elizabeth Garnett

Windows are, of course, memorials too. It is worth noting the "Faith Hope and Charity" window (nave south aisle) which was given in memory of Caroline, the wife of Charles Longley, the first bishop of Ripon, as a tribute of respect from friends and neighbours. The window shows aspects of Victorian female life: caring for the sick, reading from the Bible, and family worship.

The most recent memorial, a new suspended stained glass window in the Chapel of Justice and Peace in the north nave aisle, was dedicated to Jean Emmerson who died in 2005. Her husband Bill, gave the window in her memory. It is depicts the risen Christ and the symbolism echoes the Holy Spirit Chapel. The dedication reads, "in loving memory of Jean Emmerson. Donated by her husband Bill Emmerson". The Chapel which was converted from the former derelict and disused Consistory Court was also donated by her husband and dedicated to her.

Jean's memorial tablet in the graveyard reads simply, "In giving you God gave me everything." What a wonderful tribute. How times have changed. Here is a woman

Courtesy of Bill Emmerson

Left: Jean Emmerson who died in 2005

Right: the simple tablet to her memory in the Cathedral graveyard

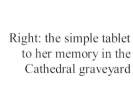

JEAN EMMERSON
1914 – 2005
IN GIVING YOU
GOD GAVE ME EVERYTHING

who is remembered for herself; how different from the Victorian tributes that were seen as the embodiment of female virtue.

Children

Childhood illnesses were far more serious and potentially fatal because of the lack of medical knowledge and modern medication, and several poignant memorials serve to remind us of the fragility of childhood. **Anna Terry** died in 1821 aged 76 while her son **William** lived only 8 years, dying in 1793.

Henry William Strickland (wall north aisle) died in 1818 aged nine, having been a boarder at the grammar school only eight days. He was ill for only a few hours before he was "taken from the world before he had known its sin or felt its sorrow". His memorial features a lovely design of five snowdrops and leaves, one having a broken stem and fallen to earth, symbolising a life cut short.
Similarly, **Henry Mills Nesfield** (wall north aisle) who had been a pupil at Bishopton School for only three weeks, died in 1823 aged 11 after a few days illness. He is remembered for his "opening virtues, sweetness of disposition, and soundness of intellect".

Above: detail from the Emmerson window. The full window is pictured on page 12

Below: detail from the Henry William Strickland plaque, the broken snowdrop symbolizing his early death

Both of these young boys were boarders, Strickland from Marnham in Nottinghamshire and Nesfield from County Durham. We should remember that being a boarder in the 19th century would not have been a pleasant experience, with poor food, straw mattresses, unhygienic conditions and corporal punishment to name only a few discomforts. The literature of the time publicised these harsh conditions, for example Dotheboys Hall in *Nicholas Nickleby* and Lowood School in *Jane Eyre*.

Sue Ford

Notes and Sources

<u>Note from the editor re dual dating:</u> The start of the year before 1752, when England finally switched to the Gregorian calendar, caused ambiguities. The

historical year starting on January 1st was in use in almanacs and celebrated in the New Year's Eve festival, however the legal (civil) New Year in England started March 25th.

Therefore the notation for dates from January 1st to March 25th was often dual, as in the memorial to Hellen Bayne in the south aisle (1694/95). The fact that she died at Easter (March 24th that year) was just a coincidence and not pertinent to the dual notation, as Easter is a movable feast. From March 25th to Dec 31st the year overlapped so there would be no need for dual notation. If she therefore had died the next day or day after that only one date would have been recorded, namely 1695.

The Christian Calendar, with which the seventeenth century population would have been familiar, could have added to the confusion. March 25th is the festival of the annunciation (Lady Day was held on March 21st and was one of the annual quarter markers when people would pay their rent and tithes etc.) and nine months later is December 25th, Christmas Day and the celebration of the birth of Christ. Some Christians consider this to be the start of the Christian Year in preference to the beginning of Advent.

The epitaph for Jean Emmerson was abridged from a poem her husband Bill wrote for her funeral.

To Jean

What can I say that others have not said?

What song remains that someone has not sung?

But this – before I thank my God for bread

I thank Him that we met when we were young

And though my praise is due for tree and flower

And each day's dawn and dusk and birds that sing.

Greater my debt grows yet – yea, hour by hour

For, giving you, God gave me everything.

We thank Dorothy Taylor for information regarding Elizabeth Garnett.

SULLIVAN, Dick: *Navvyman*, 1983

Ripon Gazette, 1875

Borthwick Institute, York

Medieval Tombs in Ripon Cathedral

The Markenfield Tombs

Three miles south of Ripon, tucked away privately down a mile-long winding drive, stands one of the most astonishing and romantic of Yorkshire's medieval houses: Markenfield - now known as Markenfield Hall, though "Hall" was added quite late in its long life.

It is still completely moated, and is the most complete surviving early fourteenth century house in England. For many centuries, it was the home of the remarkable Markenfield family until it was confiscated from them by the Crown in 1569 for High Treason, and became instead a tenanted working farm. This it remained until 1980 when the Nortons, Lords Grantley, collateral descendants of the Markenfields, moved back to live alongside the tenant farmers of the day to commence restoration of the house and estate, which is continuing.

Although the Markenfields had a beautiful domestic chapel in the heart of the house – which is still very active, and to which all are welcome – at an early stage

Markenfield Hall, built 1310 on an earlier house, home of the Markenfield family until 1569

The beautifully restored great hall and chapel seen from the entrance gateway

they established their own chantry chapel on the east side of the north transept of Ripon Cathedral, where two medieval monuments to two notable family members and their wives remain: both **Sir Thomas Markenfields,** one (d. 1398) the great-great-grandfather of the other (d.1497). They are all that is left of what must have been, before the Reformation, a very fine place of worship and family mausoleum. Numerous Markenfield family wills request that the testator be buried "afore the altar of St Andrew, among my ancestors" and doubtless many other family tombs still lie under the flagstones.

Mass would have been said here daily for the souls of the family departed, by the resident chantry priest It is probable that this was the same priest who also said Mass daily in the chapel at Markenfield itself and that he commuted between his two chapels every day. Those familiar with Yorkshire weather and muddy tracks will know this would not always have been a pleasure.

The older and finer tomb, in the centre, is of the Sir Thomas who was the doyen of the family when it was at the height of its influence and wealth. It would probably have originally carried a canopy (often referred to as a hearse), as does the similar tomb of Sir John Marmion (d.1387) in West Tanfield Church; the late John Cornforth thought the two tombs were quite probably by the same sculptor.

This Sir Thomas fought in the Hundred Year War between 1360 and 1385 and was appointed Governor of Guise in Northern France. He also held various high appointments locally, including High Steward of the Archbishop of York's Liberty of Ripon and Steward of the Earl of Derby's Lordship of Kirkby Malzeard, both of which would have helped defray his expenditure improving Markenfield as it became grander. His armour on the tomb bears the Markenfield arms in several places: (argent) on a bend (sable) three bezants (a gold coin from Byzantium, believed to

have been the most stable currency in Europe when these arms were acquired by Canon John de Markenfield in 1308).

Most curious is his unusual collar, which shows a couchant stag within an elaborate fence round a little field; an elegant design. Many learned essays have been written seeking to

Left: view of the Markenfield tomb as approached from the north transept

Effigies of Sir Thomas Markenfield (d. 1398) and his wife Dionisia

prove that this was a badge marking his adherence to the House of Lancaster; others think it is simply a play on the family's name – Mark-in-Field (a 'mark' being your quarry in a hunt) – similar to the medieval humour shown by a rebus in heraldry. [Ed: A third hypothesis links the stag couchant to the Earls of Derby.] Among the Markenfield archives, there is a sketch made on the back of a sixteenth century memorandum showing the same design as a large pendant, probably worn by members of the family.

A stag is clearly visible
on Sir Thomas' collar

Around the tomb are fifteen shields bearing the coats-of-arms of the families with whom the Markenfields were then related, usually by marriage:

1.   Fretty with a canton, for Middleton
2.   An eagle displayed impaling five fusils in fess, for Soothill
3.   Three water bougets, for Ross
4.   Blank
5.   A cross fleuree, for Ward

6. A simple bend, for Scrope
7. The same
8. A lion rampant debruised by a bend dexter, for Sutton or Slingsby
9. A canton charged with a fleur de lys, for Metham
10. On a bend three bezants, for Markenfield
11. Unclear
12. Markenfield impaling three helmets crested with fleur de lys, for Miniot(t)
13. Charged with a saltire, for Neville
14. Charged with a chevron, for Stafford
15. Three water bougets, for Ross

[Ed: Some of this heraldic detail is taken from Planché, 1864, when the tomb was perhaps less eroded.]

Next to Sir Thomas lies what remains of the image of his wife, heiress of the Miniot family of Carlton Miniott near Thirsk, whose arms are among the fifteen shields engraved round the tomb (which itself bears no inscription). We only know of her unusual Christian name - **Dionisia** – because of the survival of a rather touching certificate signed at Markenfield. By this, Sir Thomas appointed Dominus John de Fulforth as chantry chaplain to this Chapel, on 9 March 1398. To this has been added a postscript, a few days later, reading "And I, Dionisia, widow of Dominus Thomas de Markenfield, deceased, consent to the said presentation made by Thomas, who had signed it".

The monument is made of magnesian limestone, the effigies being carved from a much finer-grained material than the tomb chest. The earliest illustration, a pencil sketch made in 1669 now in the Bodleian Library, makes it clear that much of the physical destruction of Lady Markenfield's effigy had occurred by then. The damage is said to have been carried out in 1643 by soldiers of the Parliamentarian Army under the command of Mauleverer of Allerton during the Civil War, who took the figures to be "idolatrous images".

The monument of the other **Sir Thomas** now lies against the North wall, though this may not have always been its position; the fact that its East end is not only blank but very rough suggests that this face was originally against a wall. He had been seneschal of Ripon and later High Sheriff of Yorkshire. Next to him lies his wife **Eleanor**, daughter of Sir John Conyers of Hornby Castle. Although also made of magnesian limestone, it is very much coarser in appearance, leading some to believe it may have at some point stood in the Churchyard. It is now badly worn, but fortunately the Ripon antiquarian John Richard Walbran copied some details in the mid-nineteenth century. The inscription reads:

HIC JACET TOMAS M'KNEFELD MILES ET ELENOR UXOR [EJUS ILLE OBIJT PRI]MO MENC' MAIJ ANNO D['NI MCC] CCLXXXXVIJ Q FUIT SENESCHALLUS ISTI' VILLE ET KURKBI MALLZEDE ET ELENOR [OBIJT] V DIE MENC' MAIJ A D'NI MCCCCLXXXXIIJ

(Here lies Thomas Markenfield Knight and Elenor his wife. He died 1st May 1497 and was Seneschal of this place and of Kirkby Malzeard, and Elenor his wife died the 5th May 1498)

Walbran also noted the arms on the head and side of the tomb thus:

1, *a saltire*; 2, *a chevron*, 3, *a cross flory* for Ward of Givendale; 4, *a maunch* for Conyers; 5, Markenfield; and 6, *three water bougets*, probably, for Roos.

This Sir Thomas holds the unenviable distinction of being attainted twice for treason in the Wars of the Roses, being on the losing sides at both the battles of Towton (1461) and Bosworth (1485). In both cases he was pardoned, probably at considerable cost Politically tacking and weaving, as was the custom of the time, he managed to become High Sherriff of Yorkshire twice, once under a Lancastrian King and once under a Yorkist and died a distinguished old man, a credit to Yorkshire.

Thomas and Eleanor's son, Ninian, was knighted on the field at the Battle of Flodden against the Scots (9 September 1513) in the Order of the Bath, for his courage and military prowess in the best tradition of his family. He too was buried in this Chapel, as his will requested, but his grave is now unmarked.

Immediately to the west is a limestone coped coffin lid set into the flagstone floor. Walbran comments that it "probably commemorates some canon of the Minster in the 13th century. Prior to recent alterations [he wrote in 1844] it was turned face downwards"

In 2004, the two Markenfield monuments were expertly cleaned and conserved by Dr David Carrington of Skillington Workshop Ltd. An impressive dossier with photographs and diagrams recording every stage of the work has been deposited with the Chapter.

While this was in progress, the two stone conservators, Paul Wooles and Theo Gayer -Anderson, were invited to Markenfield Hall, where they immediately spotted that the house was largely built of the same magnesian limestone as had been used for the later monument if not both. This is known to have come from the quarry 600 yards east of the house, now heavily overgrown. It is touching to realise that, in spite of richer and finer stone being available to them, the later Sir Thomas and his wife and possibly his great-great-grandfather chose rather to be commemorated in stone from their beloved home.

The most remarkable and memorable member of the Markenfield family was not, alas, buried in this Chapel though he would dearly have liked to be. He was another Sir Thomas, the last of the family to live at Markenfield. A passionate and devout Catholic, he embarked on a pilgrimage to Jerusalem in 1566 when he was 23 – an arduous and dangerous journey at the best of times, but in that year made extra hazardous by the savage warfare between Islam and Christianity which engulfed the Mediterranean, following the Great Siege of Malta.

Soon after his return, Thomas became the central figure in the Rising of the North; many believe he was the main instigator. This was the Catholic rising against Protestant Queen Elizabeth and an attempt to restore Catholic freedom of worship to the North. A large contingent of the Rising gathered in the courtyard at Markenfield on 20th November 1569, under Thomas and his uncle, the venerable Sir Richard Norton of Norton Conyers, High Sheriff of Yorkshire. He was the standard bearer, and carried the Rising's banner of the Five Wounds of Christ, a great white crucifix on his breast "his white hair streaming in the wind, and his face fired with high enthusiasm for what he deemed a holy and sacred cause."

Having heard Mass in the Chapel at Markenfield, the leaders rode out at the head of a large host here to Ripon Minster, where they overturned the high altar, burned the new Protestant Prayer Books and held a solemn high Mass. It is most probable that young Sir Thomas went to this Chantry Chapel of his ancestors during that tumultuous day and prayed at these and other, no longer extant, family tombs, for something of their military prowess for the battles that lay ahead.

Alas, the Rising was routed and the lucky ones, including Thomas and "Old Norton", as his uncle Richard was known, managed to flee. Over two hundred of their followers were caught and hideously executed. Thomas and Richard waited for a while in Scotland with other rebels, but as the net closed around them there, they had to flee again across the North Sea to the Low Countries, where they somehow survived in increasing poverty.

On 21 April 1570, two Commissioners arrived in Yorkshire to survey Markenfield for Robert Cecil, Secretary of State to Queen Elizabeth, the new owner. Their report survives, and describes the house much as it is now. It then stood empty, and was soon to be downgraded from a noble house to a tenanted working farm with an absentee landlord.

In May 1576, Cardinal Como wrote to the Bishop of Liége, to say that the Pope had been "moved to compassion by the great indigence to which an English nobleman, Sir Thomas Markenfield, was now reduced" and requesting that he be taken in and looked after by some wealthy monastery.

Old Sir Richard was shot in a skirmish, when he was taken prisoner by English soldiers in Flanders. He died of his injuries at sea on 9th April 1585, whilst being taken back to England to imprisonment or execution. His Will was made on board on the day of his death, and in it he left ten French crowns to the ordinary sailors who were looking after him with gentleness and consideration.

For whatever reason, Sir Thomas was not taken into a monastery. His wife Isabel Ingleby (Ingilby) of Ripley Castle had been allowed to stay on at Markenfield in 1569, to look after their young son Ninian – probably in the cluster of hovels just south of the present farm buildings. A friend wrote to Thomas on 19 March 1593 with news: "Your wife is poor, but prayeth hard for you....I fear she is in great lack of worldly comforts".

Unknown to this correspondent, Thomas had already died. In August 1592, a papal correspondent Richard Verstagan had written that "Sir Thomas Markenfield has been found dead, lying on the bare floor of his chamber, no creature being present at his death.....He died this last week in Brussels, in very extreme want and in a most miserable cottage". His grave is unknown. Perhaps among his last thoughts were his beloved Markenfield and his family Chantry Chapel in Ripon Cathedral, where he too would be resting in peace but for this catastrophe.

The last of the family, Elizabeth, Ninian's widow and Thomas's daughter-in-law, continued to live alone, probably in the fields South of the house. Under different circumstances, she would have been mistress of Markenfield and buried here in the family Chantry Chapel; but the end of the story was very different. It is to be found in the parish registers of Ripon Cathedral, which record that "Elizabeth Markenfield of Markenfield, widow" was given a pauper's burial on 4 October 1600.

Ian Curteis

Notes and Sources

A Requiem Mass for these last four Markenfields is now held every August in the Chapel at Markenfield. It is a Catholic Chapel, at which Anglican services are welcome. Please contact the administrator for details of both Catholic and Anglican services.

The House itself is usually open to the public every afternoon during the first fortnight of May and the second fortnight of June. Guided tours may be arranged at any time of year. The administrator will gladly provide more details (01765 692303).

SHEPPARD ROUTH, Pauline & KNOWLES Richard: " *The Markenfield Collar"*, in *The Yorkshire Archaeological Journal* vol. 62, (1990)

Note from the editor:

Brian Crosse has put forward an interesting theory with regard to the stag collar. A stag was the badge of King Richard II and later the Yorkist Edward IV, whereas the Lancastrian kings had, as one of their badges, a heraldic antelope – a very different beast. This seems to undermine the theory that Sir Thomas's collar with the stag couchant was indicative of Lancastrian sympathies. Could the stag behind palings have been symbolic of a desire to imprison Richard II?

Rich landowners endowed chantry chapels so that masses could be celebrated for the landowner's well-being on earth and his soul after death. Some were endowed by guilds and religious societies for the benefit of their members. Before the dissolution of the chantries in 1547, it was recorded that Ripon Minster had at least nine chantry chapels, however throughout the latter Middle Ages this number may have varied. It appears that, then as now, inflation took its toll on a number of endowments. Upon dissolution, the revenues to support the chantry chapels in Ripon were added to the possessions of the Duchy of Lancaster. (Thanks to J. Paul Burbridge for information regarding Chantry Chapels in Ripon Minster.)

The Ripon Chapter MS (Grant of Lands for a Chantry), Surtees Society, Vol.74, p.153, records that a Johannes de Markyngfeld, Canon of York, in 1319 endowed a chantry priest, Richard of Linton, to do divine service for the soul of Aunger of Ripon. It is assumed that this Markenfield Chantry shared the east side of the north transept with the Chantry of St Andrew which was probably founded in 1234 (or 1369 according to a visitation document) by Geoffrey de Larder and David de Wollore, sometime Canons of Ripon Minster (and perhaps re-endowed in 1369).

The Lion Tomb

The Cathedral at Ripon has still not given up all its mysteries, with one memorial in particular being the focus of much speculation.

In the south aisle of the nave, close to the font, is an old stone monument fixed to the outer south wall. At first glance it may appear totally blank of decoration or inscription and could be mistaken for a small altar or stone table. Closer examination of the grey stone top shows an incised panel on the eastern-most end. The inscription on the base of the tomb unfortunately has become illegible. Both the top and the base of this monument are made of local Yorkshire magnesian limestone.

The Lion Tomb in 2008. The inscription on the front panel is now illegible but due reverence is shown the memorial by the routing of the heating pipe around it!

Above: 2008 photo of the top end panel of the Lion tomb showing the worn image of a lion and a man

Above: Hallett in 1901 published this rubbing from the top panel

Below: an inaccurate etching from a Cathedral inventory of 1847

Although subject to progressively debilitating wear over the past several hundreds of years, the incised panel is still recognisable as the representation of a large lion standing in a plant/tree filled background, among whose branches is a perching bird. At the right hand edge of the panel is a kneeling human figure, generally taken to be a young man, wearing a knee length loosely fitting robe.

The history of this composite memorial – assembled from at least two separate items of differing antiquity – is clouded in mystery, with an 18th century description offering a colourful explanation:

"There stands hard by the font, an altar-tomb covered with a slab of grey marble, on the horizontal surface of which is sculptured, in low relief, the representation of a man and a lion in a grove of trees, and concealing some wild tale in a black letter inscription that time has irretrievably mouldered from the vertical stone below. A century ago, tradition recounted that it covered the body of an Irish Prince, who died at Ripon on his return from Palestine, whence he had brought a lion that followed him with all the docility and faithfulness of a spaniel."—Walbran's *Ripon and Harrogate*, 1777.

Some have suggested that its use was that of a bargaining or money table by local trades-people. During the Middle Ages the nave was used as a social meeting place for locals, not just as a place for worship. Is this the table where perhaps business deals were sealed?

Or was the base a disused chantry altar? In the 16th century chantry chapels were removed from Churches and the altars would have become redundant.

There are few claims that this is a true memorial to an individual or to a family, although at least one writer has suggested that it may be linked to a 14th century family from Topcliffe in North Yorkshire. This putative link has been derived from the similarities of style of the Ripon monument's lion and plants to those of the brass of Thomas de Topcliffe in Topcliffe parish Church. The design of both the brass and the incised slab on the lion-tomb are thought to be of late 14th century Flemish origin. It has been argued that the same craftsmen sometimes worked brass and stone and that during the later Middle Ages Flemish immigrants worked in English workshops. However, without further evidence we shall never know if there is indeed a link with the Topcliffe Brass (1391).

What makes this monument even more of a conundrum is the fact that it was added to the south aisle after the extension of the nave in the early 1500s. It was in fact built onto the stone ledging provided along the outer wall of the south aisle. The base too could predate this period as it shows extensive wearing, perhaps due to it having been weathered whilst outside the Cathedral.

Therefore, if the carving is of 14th century origin, it was fitted onto the base of the tomb at a much later date. The style of the base certainly is of a much later architectural style than the carved tabletop. This begs the question of the original purpose of the carved slab and why it was reused on this tomb. Thus we must look to the iconography for further clues.

In part due to the poor visibility of the decorative carving, and in part due to repetition of the error by others, the most familiar illustration of this monument is from an inventory of the memorials assembled in 1847 by the then Cathedral Sexton. Unfortunately his illustration is based on crude etching executed with minimal regard to the original subject matter. (The head of his lion is a grotesque, the kneeling figure is a very loose approximation and the background is not accurately portrayed!) [see pictures on page 35]

A more correct visualisation from an actual rubbing of the *bas relief* sculpture is included in a description of the Cathedral by Hallett in 1901. Despite the benefit of greater accuracy in the illustration, Hallett – like others before him – is unable to provide historic sources for this tomb.

Over the years, the iconography has been linked to various stories: the returning Irish prince (see above), to the life of St Jerome – often portrayed with a lion; or more recently even to St Paul the Hermit.

This latter hypothesis bases itself on a 3rd century Christian who lived in the deserts of Egypt to avoid persecution. His daily bread was brought to him by a raven and on his death he was found in a kneeling pose, head turned heavenward while lions appeared and dug his grave! Apparently St Paul the Hermit lived on the bread brought by the bird and on fruits of the plants around him.

Whilst this last interpretation is appealing, some experts have argued that the medieval clothing of the kneeling figure is that of a secular person and not one in holy orders, although a fashion guide for hermits has never been published. And so the arguments continue...

Andrew Coulson

Notes and Sources

GREENHILL, F.A.: *"The Ripon Lion"*, in Transactions of the Monumental Brass Society, **10,** (1963-68)

HALLETT, C.: *The Cathedral church of Ripon: a short history of the church and a description of its fabric"*, London

SMITH, Lucius: *The Story of Ripon Minster*, (1912)

WILSON, T.: "*A verbatim copy of all the monuments, gravestones and other sepulchral memorials in Ripon Cathedral and its burial ground."* (1847)

Memorials to Clergymen

It would be strange if the clergy who have served this great Church were not well represented among its memorials. It is unfortunate that – unlike other Cathedrals and Minsters – only one such memorial survives from the medieval period. In the south choir aisle there is a by now largely illegible brass plate commemorating **John Deen** (Dene) Residentiary Canon of Ripon Minster and Prebendary of Stanwiggs (now Stanwick). It is assumed that the plaque was fitted during his lifetime as the date of death has never been filled in but left blank. His will and other sources, however, place his death sometime between 1433 and 1435. During the Middle Ages the role of the Prebendary of Stanwick was usually combined with that of the Cathedral Precentor (the Canon in charge of directing the services and the liturgical / musical aspects of worship).

The earliest post-medieval memorial is that of Dean **Moses Fowler** (1608) in the south choir aisle; a good example of its period. Just as the last Abbot of Fountains survived the Reformation to become the first minister of the newly created parish Church, so Fowler made a similar transition from incumbent to Dean of the restored collegiate foundation under James I's charter in 1604. He did not survive long; his (truncated) figure now lies atop his wall monument, with members of his family once kneeling below on either side of a desk, a common type of that period. The figures have vanished and the monument bears witness to the damage done to the Cathedral soon after its erection, but its epitaph still proudly survives (here in translation), thanks to his son Daniel and his wife Jane whose will credits them with the restoration of the memorial –

Heav'n, Earth and mortals all contend the same –
Which of the three shall champion FOWLER'S name.
But see a Heav'n sent messenger descend
And judgement give how this dispute shall end.
His soul he gave to Heav'n, to Earth his frame,
To us immortal tokens of his fame

It is a pity that Daniel and Jane's restoration could not have been more thorough!

Anthony Higgin, Fowler's successor as Dean, was even more unfortunate – all that survives of his monument, (reminiscent of the famous Shakespeare bust at Stratford), is a headless bust in a wall memorial in the Library (1624), which fell victim to the Parliamentarian troops under Mauleverer in 1643. Its position does, however, recall the great benefaction that Higgin made to the Minster: the impressive collection of books which filled what had been the medieval Lady Loft above the Chapter House. Higgin in his undergraduate days at Cambridge was a contemporary of the Elizabethan playwright Richard Greene; by the time he came to Ripon, he was a collector on no mean scale. Between 1615 and 1622 he donated no less than 758 books, mainly theological and historical, to his Minster Church, and the Lady Loft, which had already contained a small medieval collection in its pre-Reformation days, must have seemed the best repository. One wonders how some of these treasures, now deposited with the Brotherton Library in Leeds University, survived, considering the fate of Dean Higgin's memorial.

Headless bust of Dean Anthony Higgin

By the eighteenth century clerical memorials were in no such danger. In the Chapter House a large wall plaque of white marble against a grey background, taking the form of a classical sarcophagus in relief over a florid inscription, now in English as opposed to the earlier Latin, commemorates one of the more notable Deans of that period, **Robert Darley Waddilove** (1828). His is an interesting story, illustrating well the career ladder of eighteenth century dignitaries. Born a Darley in Boroughbridge, he inherited property there from an uncle, whose name he adopted, and at first dithered between a career in law and the Church. Later he became Chaplain to the English Ambassador to Spain, Lord Grantham, (where he pursued literary occupations in the Escorial Library), and to Archbishops Drummond and Markham of York, while holding livings at Whitby then Topcliffe. He became a Prebendary, first of Ripon and then also of York, before becoming eventually Archdeacon of the East Riding (1786) and then Dean of Ripon in 1792, posts he held concurrently until his death in 1828 at the age of 92. Pluralism was not uncommon in those days, so Ripon may well have seen little of its much-travelled Dean, who was also a magistrate, although his epitaph (probably composed by himself) seeks to reassure us that *'his attention and*

Marble wall plaque to Dean Robert Darley Waddilove

his assiduity in the duties of his station were as remarkable as they were constant and sincere.' The florid language of that period lends a certain irony to that statement. There is a monument to his wife (1797) in the Chapter House and others to a daughter and two grandsons in the north transept. Another daughter married into the Oxley family of what is now Minster House, whose own memorials can be seen in the south-west tower. As if this were not enough, there is also a window to Dean Waddilove in the south nave aisle and to other members of his extended family, inserted later in the nineteenth century.

In stark contrast to his predecessor and his family, the sole memorial to Dean **James Webber** (1847) is his name on the painted list of Deans in the south-west tower. He deserves better as he became the first Dean of the new Cathedral foundation when the Diocese of Ripon was set up in 1836. More substantial is that to his children, listed upon a marble stele-type wall memorial in St Peter's Chapel (north choir aisle). It commemorates (in elegant Latin) first of all his second daughter **Jemima** who died in 1840 at the age of 14 and was buried on the north side of the altar. She also inspired a quotation from the Italian poet Tasso (from his *Jerusalem Delivered*) in the original language. Here it is, in translation, with the original Italian engraving:

> Now you live in bliss; for our own future lot,
> not your misfortune, tempts us with tears, since,
> with your passing, so deserving and considerable
> a part of us goes with you.
> But if that, which in common terms is known as Death
> has deprived us of an aid on earth, you may beseech
> on our behalf celestial aid, now that
> Heaven has received you amidst the chosen.

> VIVI BEATA PUR ; CHÈ NOSTRA SORTE ,
> NON TU SVENTURA A LAGRIMAR N'INVITA ;
> POSCIACH'AL TUO PARTIR SÌ DEGNA E FORTE
> PARTE DI NOI FA COL TUO PIÈ PARTITA .
> MA SE QUESTA, CHE'L VOLGO APPELLA MORTE,
> PRIVATI HA NOI D'UNA TERRENA AÌTA ;
> CELESTE AÌTA ORA IMPETRAR NE PUOI ,
> CHE'L CIEL T'ACCOGLIE INFRA GLI ELETTI SUOI.

All her brothers and sister are also listed and there unfolds a tragic story of this Dean's family. **Cyril** died in 1831, aged 17, as the result of a sudden fall. Then his younger brother **Edward** drowned in the Thames in 1833 at the age of 15 – was he perhaps at Eton? Two years after the Dean died, his son **Charles** was killed unexpectedly by a *'machinæ ictu igniferæ'* – opinions differ as to whether this was a steam engine or a railway train. The final entry, Jemima's elder sister, **Caroline Maria** carries the greatest pathos: she was the first to die, in infancy, 'in her cot', perhaps the earliest reference to a 'cot death'. Since he is also recorded, we probably owe this family memorial to the Dean's eldest son who died at the age of 65 in 1881, while in Switzerland. He himself was ordained and became Minor Canon and Sub-Dean of St Paul's Cathedral, where he displayed musical talent.

After the elevation of the Minster to be the Cathedral Church of the new diocese, glass became the favoured medium for clerical memorials. The great west window (1886) commemorates the first two bishops: **Charles Longley** went on to become Bishop of Durham, Archbishop of York and finally of Canterbury, where he inaugurated the Lambeth Conferences. **Robert Bickersteth**, (1884) the second bishop began a family succession of bishops: Edward, of Exeter, Edward, of South Tokyo and, more recently, John, of Bath and Wells. There are other windows to members of the families of these two bishops. Stone tablets are rarer, but there is an interesting coloured alabaster tablet to Dean **William Fremantle** (1916). He was an important figure on the liberal wing of Anglicanism and became involved in controversy over the doctrine of the Virgin Birth.

Detail from the West Window, part of the memorial to Bishops Longley and Bickersteth

Bishops, Deans and Canons are buried in the Cathedral graveyard, but in the last half century there has been a swing back to interior memorials, not least of a practical as well as commemorative nature. Dean **Mansfield Owen**, to whose efforts we owe the fine Reredos, is himself commemorated (1941) by the three standing coloured figures of Our Lady with Archbishops Roger de Pont l'Evêque and Walter de Grey above the south choir aisle entrance. He and Dean **Birchenough** have also been given carved

This group of three figures commemorates Dean Mansfield Owen

inscriptions, with their coats of arms, in the wall of the Chapel of the Holy Spirit, beside Dean Fowler's memorial.

The most striking modern memorial is that to Bishop **John Moorman** (1989), one of the greatest scholars and ecumenical figures of the Church of England in the last century. A worn mediaeval tub font, probably from the time of Archbishop Roger Pont l'Evêque, has been mounted on a low stone block and capped with a circular plate glass table top to form the altar of St Peter's Chapel in the north choir aisle. The glass is engraved with the inscription "that they may all be one" (*John 17.11*), recalling the two great sacraments of Christian unity and Bishop Moorman's work with the Second Vatican Council and the

This medieval font is now an alter in memory of Bishop John Moorman

setting up of the Anglican Centre in Rome. One of the most noted authorities on St Francis, his great library is now at St Deiniol's Library in North Wales.

Dean **Llewelyn Hughes,** who served under Bishop Moorman until 1968, has an equally appropriate memorial: an oval slate plaque is mounted in the right hand wall of the forecourt of the Cathedral, recording the fact that it was restored in his memory. Dean Hughes came to Ripon in 1951, having served as Chaplain-General to the Armed Forces, and before that with the 8th Army in Italy and 1st Army in NW Europe under Field Marshal Montgomery during the last years of the Second World War. The last Dean to live in The Residence, he is still remembered in Ripon above all for his pastoral care of the Cathedral parish and his approachability, he and his wife keeping a warm welcome in their home for their parishioners. He was not above bringing his guitar into the pulpit to enliven worship, a precursor of what was to come in the Church. It is a fitting tribute that his memorial should be the welcoming open space to the Cathedral with its information boards and stone bordering wall and he would have approved its subsequent elegant repaving, with improved access for the disabled.

Under Dean Birchenough the Chapel of the Resurrection, to the east of the Song School and with its own entry under the Chapter House, was restored in 1948 and refurnished and rededicated under Bishop David Young in 1984 for worship and private prayer. This simple vaulted undercroft is one of the oldest corners of the Cathedral. In its second restoration it was given its circular altar, formed from the section of a column recovered from the foundations of the Anglo-Saxon Minster, as a memorial to Bishop **Stuart Hetley Price** who died tragically from cancer after only nine months as Bishop in succession to John Moorman. Formerly Bishop of Doncaster before he came to Ripon, his ashes are interred in a wall nearby, as are those of other clergy and laity who have served this foundation, while those of Dean **Godwin Birchenough** (1953) lie under a finely incised and inscribed lozenge stone before the altar.

A more recent interment inscription is that of **John G. Williams** (2000), Honorary Minor Canon of the Cathedral during his retirement, caring for St John, Bondgate, and Littlethorpe. He had previously had a ministry as a parish priest, a distinguished author and religious broadcaster with the BBC during the Second World War, and later with the SPCK as Editor and Education Officer, so the Cathedral continues its long tradition of recalling to mind those who have served its ministry as well as in the wider community.

Floor and wall plaques commemorating Dean Birchenough and the Rev. John Williams

David Murfet

Notes and Sources

We thank Canon Keith Punshon for pointing out the medieval brass of John Dene

For the will of John Dene see: *Memorials of Ripon*, Surtees Society, Vol. 78, p. 249

Dictionary of National Biography (for individual clerics)

SMITH, Lucius: *The Story of Ripon Minster*, (1912)

The papers of the Surtees and Yorkshire Archaeological Societies

The 17th Century

$$1 6 9 \frac{4}{5}$$

Jordan Crosland

Jordan Crosland was born in Helmsley, in North Yorkshire, in 1617. He was the son of John Crosland (II), who was a steward and agent for the northern manors of the 5th Earl of Rutland, as his father had been before him. Of a family of ten children, Jordan was one of only five who survived beyond the age of twenty years. John Crosland had achieved a position of some importance by the time he died in 1635. Francis, the eldest son, died a year later and Jordan became the "man of the house".

At this point, the storm of the Civil War broke upon the land. This dashing young man of eighteen years, Royalist in sympathy, joined King Charles and was knighted at Lincoln at the age of twenty-three. All this was in the splendid tradition of the young Cavalier riding off to war winning glory in the field.

He rose rapidly in the ranks of the King's men and, as a young colonel, he was made Governor of Helmsley Castle. In 1644, the castle was held to siege by Sir Thomas Fairfax and his Parliamentary forces. Crosland held out for three months, but the lack of food and water forced him to agree to surrender. Whether it was the esteem in which he was held, his negotiating skills or the high degree of chivalry with which, some of the time, this war was conducted, he and his garrison were given honourable terms.

Extract from the Terms of Surrender

Propositions desired by Colonell Crosland Governour of Helmesley Castle concerninge the Surrenderinge thereof:

That the Governour of the castle and all other the officers shall march out with their Armes, horses, and all the rest of their goode belonginge unto them, and to be safely convoy'd to the Garrison at Scarborough without aine molestacon. That the souldyers shall march out with their Armes loaden, matches lighted, colours flyinge, and drums beateinge, and to be safely convoyed to the said garrison...

Courtesy of Rachael Fox-Evans

Ruins of Helmsley Castle in 2008

In 1642, as a "Royalist Traitor", Jordan Crosland faced accusations of being a "Papist" (Catholic) and the loss of his estates. The Catholic brothers of his wife also had to fight for their land and more than one document of the time deals with the sequestration of their property. In one of these, Crosland is described as a "recusant (Catholic) and delinquent", which he denied, although later on in life he was to become a devout Catholic. Already his grandfather had been charged with recusancy. It was common at this time for Catholic heirs of estates to attend Anglican services or even to be brought up as Anglicans to avoid the stiff financial penalties for not conforming (they were known as "Church Papists"). Jordan's wife Bridget is also on record for sending a petition to the government commissioners in the ongoing battle for her family's estate. In the end both families managed to salvage some property and their fortunes took an upturn in 1660 upon the Restoration of the Monarchy.

Sir Jordan Crosland became governor of Scarborough Castle for the period of 1665/66 and commander of trained bands in Yorkshire. The residence of Sir Jordan and his family, in the castle, gave the town its first Catholic gentry for many years.

In 1665, George Fox, considered the founder of the Quaker Movement, was imprisoned in the Castle. He often debated with "papists" including Sir Jordan, his wife, Bridget Fleming of Ryedale in Westmoreland, and his priest. Fox declared: "Crosland treated me very lovingly and said that whatever he could do for my Friends he would do it and never hurt them." George Fox earned great respect from Sir Jordan, who described him as "stiff as a tree and pure as a bell." When Fox was released by the King, the following passport was issued by Sir Jordan Crosland. "Permit the bearer hereof, George Fox, late a prisoner here but now discharged by His Majesty's order, quietly to pass about his lawful occasions without molestation. Given under my hand at Scarborough Castle this 1st day of September 1666." As a result of the empathy between Fox and Crosland, Quakers and Catholics seem to have co-existed peacefully in Scarborough and surroundings. In 1661 Jordan Crosland also became Member of Parliament for the Borough of Scarborough.

Later on in life, Sir Jordan moved to Newby Hall near Ripon. He died in 1670 at the age of 53 years, a well-loved and honoured man and was buried in Ripon Cathedral with great ceremony and acclaim.

Brass memorial to Jordan Crosland

His widow and family continued to live at Newby Hall until, in 1689, his eldest surviving son, John (IV), sold the house to Sir Edward Blackett, who promptly demolished it and built the estate we see today.

Three of his other sons took Holy Orders: George as a secular priest, Charles as a Jesuit and Henry as a Dominican. In 1693 Lady Crosland entered a Benedictine convent in Cambrai, in Belgium, together with two of her grand-daughters, aged 11 and 14 years. She died there aged 90 years.

Sir Jordan Crosland was a hero in the style of all the best historical novels; the difference being that he actually existed and fought for his King with fervour and devotion.

An English translation of this Latin epitaph in the south transept of the Cathedral reads:

TO GOD THE BEST THE GREATEST
JORDAN CROSLAND OF NEWBY
CONSTABLE OF SCARBOROUGH AND
DEFENDER AND RETAINER OF THE CASTLE
COLONEL IN THE REIGNS OF CHARLES I AND CHARLES II
WHO LIVED WITH GREAT PRAISE
AND DIED WITH EQUAL GLORY
20TH AUGUST
IN THE YEAR OF OUR VIRGIN'S OFFSPRING 1670
AT THE AGE OF 53

DUTIFUL TO GOD AND FAITHFUL TO THE KING
TRUSTWORTHY TO HIS COUNTRY
NO ONE WAS MORE LOYAL TO HIS COUNTRY OR BRAVER IN ARMS
TO GUARD THE SACRED LAWS OF THE ROYAL HOUSE
OFTEN HE SET OUT UNDAUNTED INTO THE MIDST OF BATTLES
WHEN PEOPLE WERE REBELLING, CARRIED ALONG BY THE KING'S LOVE
NO ONE THUNDERED MORE IN WAR
NO ONE WAS MORE REPOSED IN PEACE
TERRIBLE IN HIS HELMET, MATURE IN ASSEMBLY
HE WAS UNSPOILT BY THE FAME OF LIFE
THIS DISTINGUISHED MAN ADORNS WITH PERPETUAL BRILLIANCE
THIS MONUMENT BY HIS HONOURABLE DEATH.

Frances Demain

Notes and Sources

Research from primary sources by Andrew Coulson

Ripon Millenary Record, 1892

A History of Helmsley, Rivaulx and District, (Members of the Helmsley and Area Group of the Yorkshire Archaeological Society) The Stonegate Press, Leeds, 1963

Terms of Surrender of Helmsley Castle (British Museum, Add MS 18979)

http://www.rootsweb.com/~englan/1642indexRoyalists.htm

'Townships: Church Coniston', *A History of the County of Lancaster.* Volume 8, 1914

Robert Dawson

Before his death on 22nd March 1604, **Robert Dawson** was a wealthy landowner like his father Gilbert Dawson of Azerley. Born in 1571 or 1572, he was the Sheriff of York for some time, but spent the last few years of his life in Ripon, where he owned and managed a portfolio of properties in the Ripon area. Much of this land had belonged to the Church prebends and chantries before it was diverted into the hands of the Crown during the Reformation. For example, shortly after Dawson came to Ripon, a document dated 1599 formalises the lease of the property of the former prebends of Stanwick, Thorpe, Sharow, Nunwick, Givendale and Monkton to Robert Dawson. Robert Dawson collected the rents and tithes from these agricultural and residential holdings, and in some cases passed the profits on to the Crown through the agency of the Duchy of Lancaster.

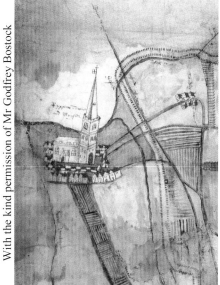

West Yorkshire Archive Service, Leeds, WYL607/31
With the kind permission of Mr Godfrey Bostock

To use an early seventeenth century term, Robert Dawson was a fee farmer, following in the footsteps of his father Gilbert. In the early seventeenth century this meant that he collected rent on behalf of the land owner. His memorial has been widely interpreted to describe him as

'RipponTowne and Mynster' on a map painted during Robert Dawson's lifetime. (Part of a larger map showing the Honour of Kirkby Malzeard attributed to Greenhurst & Browne, ca. 1600)

the "former chief of Rippon Church", but "farmer" chief is perhaps more accurate – as he was never an ecclesiastical leader.

If Robert Dawson had still been alive in 1604, it seems probable that he (like those who survived him) would have dug his heels in and refused to adhere to the terms of James I's Charter, which required the Duchy of Lancaster and private owners to return the prebendal lands in order to fund the re-establishment of the Collegiate Church. This reluctance of land owners to return property to the Church forced the writing of a further two charters in 1607 and 1610, as well as the diversion of Crown funds from elsewhere to fund re-establishment.

He certainly benefited financially from his management of chantry and prebendal lands but his memorial promotes the impression that his relationship with the Church was not simply pecuniary. Engraved upon the brass strips, which nineteenth century sources suggest once surrounded his stone bust, is a description of "his minde devout", and it is known that he wanted to be buried in the Church at Ripon: "within the quier there, neere my children." His memorial also tells us that he followed the long held custom of giving money to the less well off: "his wealth the poore well fedd". It is impossible to know if he did this for altruistic reasons, or as a way of ensuring a place in Heaven.

It is equally difficult to gauge how he felt about the Church, as there is no evidence that he ever used his wealth to support either the fabric or the teaching of the Minster, even though circa 1600 the windows were decayed and the stone walls were in desperate need of repair. Unlike several other rich locals, he did not assist Moses Fowler by funding his first trip to London in pursuit of the Charter in 1603. When he first came to Ripon from York the Church here was in a post-Reformation state of chaos, where the clergy were limited in number and made little attempt to lead worship properly. However, there is nothing to suggest that this spiritual and moral decline worried him, and one source from around 1600 even refers to parishioners complaining about Robert Dawson himself. It is uncertain whether his rent collection tactics were seen as over-zealous or whether it was he who was accused of removing bells and other valuable items from the Church at this time.

Robert Dawson was both literate and numerate, with at least a good working knowledge of the legalities of property transactions such as leases and covenants. However, he was far from being merely a bailiff with an understanding of conveyancing; instead he was a wealthy and therefore influential landowner who was on familiar terms with local leaders, both secular and spiritual. The parish register lists Robert Dawson's occupation as "*generosus*", meaning he was of noble birth. Other *generosi* of the period were named as Mallories, Nortons, Staveleys and Burtons and it is reasonable to assume that he numbered them within his list of acquaintances and moved within elevated social circles. One of the executors of his will was Christopher Lyndall, who became first prebendary in 1604; beneficiary Anthony Taylor became Ripon's second Mayor.

Unlike many others in the upper echelons of Ripon society of the time, Robert Dawson does not seem to have held office as either a cleric or town dignitary. However, in common with all residents, he was bound by the rules of the Archbishop of York's Towne Book of 1598: for example, he could be fined 6d if a door or window was left unlocked at night; he could only buy corn in the Market Place after the bell was rung and could not let his livestock stray beyond the designated common lands.

When Robert Dawson died in 1604 he left substantial parcels of land to his sons as well as "freehold land and leases" to two of his friends or associates. His two younger sons were bequeathed: "the house at York", "land and leases at Bishop Monkton" and "the lease at Staunwicke, paying the King's rent". Before this date, he had passed much of his own property to his oldest son, George, including the Aismunderby estates and three of the prebendal houses or mansions. It is assumed to be in one of these that King James I stayed during his short visit to Ripon in 1617 "at the house of George Dawson".

It is not known of what Robert Dawson died, but it is likely that he knew his time was up, because he made time to write a will in the months immediately prior to his demise. He left behind him in Ripon three surviving children and a widow. At least three of his descendants and a family servant died during the plague which carried off over 90 Ripon people in 1625.

All that remains now of Robert Dawson are seven out of the eight original brasses that once bordered a stone memorial. The eulogy is fascinating for its unusual and somewhat earthy humour! Perhaps this is an example of how Yorkshire folk are proud of the way they are known to call a spade a spade – and presumably it was a spade that dug Robert Dawson's "fatal bed"!

Brass strips from the lost memorial to Robert Dawson. An interpretation of the original eight strips is given on the next page

49

His nature mild, his mind devout,
His wealth the poor well fed,
So dead, he lives in spite of death
And grave, his fatal bed.
Whom lately Sheriff, Mercheant free,
York's wealthy city had;
And former chief of Rippon Church,
Now Rippon mould hath clad.

Kirsty Hallett

Notes and Sources:

Archives of the Chapter of Ripon Cathedral at the Brotherton Library, University of Leeds.

Hugh Ripley

On the north nave wall immediately to the west of the crossing is the imposing memorial to **Hugh Ripley**. As one of Ripon's leading figures of the early 17th century he contributed in several ways to the City. Born in 1553, he became a merchant and mercer in Ripon, being elected Wakeman in 1604.

Memorial to
Hugh Ripley - detail

The role of Wakeman has been traced back to the 14th century, and there are records of the name Ripley holding this post in 1480, when a John Ripley was Wakeman. The duties varied over the years, but essentially the Wakeman was appointed to be responsible for the security of the people and their property once the "night watch" had been set. This is still set in Ripon every night at 9 p.m. by the Hornblower.

During 1604, Hugh Ripley worked to obtain a Charter (granted in 1604) to create a Mayoralty for Ripon. As a result he became the first Mayor at the age of 51 and in this role was supported by 12 elected aldermen and 24 councillors to oversee matters in Ripon. He served the community again as mayor in 1616/17 and 1630/31, his last period of service being at the age of 77. Hugh Ripley died in 1637, aged 84 years and is still held in high regard by the people of Ripon. His memorial dates from the late 1630s, although in its present form it is nearly 100 years younger!

The epitaph reads:

Here lieth intombed the bodie of Hvgh Ripley, late of this towne, Marcheant, who was the last Wakeman, & thrice Maior, by whose good endeavours this towne first became a Maioralite, & lived to the age of 84 yeeres, & died in the yeere of our Lord 1637.

Others seeke titles to their tombes,
Thy deeds to thy name prove new wombes,
And scvtcheons to deck their herse,
Which thou need'st not take teares and veres.
If I shovld praise thy thriving witt,
Or thy weigh'd jvdgement seasoning it,
Thy eaven & thy like straight ends,
Thy pietie to God and friends,
Thy last wovld still the greatest be
And yet all ioyntly less then the
Thov stvdiest conscience more than fame,
Still to thy gathred selfe the same.
Thy gold was not thy Saint nor wealth
Pvrchas'd by rapine worse then stealth,
Nor didst thov brooding o'er it sit.
Not doeing good till death with it.
This men may blvsh at when they see,
What thy deeds were, what theirs shovld be.
Thovrt gone before, and I waite now,
T' expect my when and make my how,
Which if my Jesus grant like thine,
Who wets my grave s'noe friend of mine.

The former monument having been defaced in the time of the civil wars, this was erected by the Corporation, A. D. MDCCXXX (1730)

Andrew Coulson

Notes and Sources

TAYLOR, M.H.: *An illustrated history of Ripon* (2005)

The Great and the Sometimes Not So Good

John Aislabie (1670 – 1742)

John Aislabie, the disgraced politician and garden designer, is remembered primarily for his involvement in the "South Sea Bubble" and for creating the water garden at Studley Royal, near Ripon.

In his youth, the well-connected Aislabie (his father George married into the highly influential Mallorie/ Mallory family), studied at Cambridge. He developed an interest in landscaping upon inheriting the Studley estate from his mother's family.

Aislabie was elected as a Member of Parliament for Ripon in 1695. Despite his Whig sympathies, he was appointed a Lord of the Admiralty in the Tory administration from 1710. His career really took off though when the Whigs were returned to office in 1714. He was made Treasurer of the Navy, and in 1718, Chancellor of the Exchequer.

In 1719 the South Sea Company proposed a deal whereby it would take over the national debt in exchange for government bonds. The company had hoped to develop a monopoly in the slave trade and benefit from exclusive trading rights in the South Seas. Aislabie was a very strong supporter of this scheme and guided the Bill through the House of Commons. The sale of shares in this company took off. The war against Spain in 1718, however, put a heavy strain on shipping and soon the company was in great trouble. "The South Sea Bubble" became one of history's worst financial scandals. When the management realized that collapse was inevitable they sold off all their personal holdings, so it was left to thousands of ordinary investors to carry the heavy losses. Many people were ruined.

John Aislabie resigned from the Exchequer in January 1721, but this did not put an end to his troubles. He was found guilty by a House of Commons investigation of the "most notorious, dangerous and infamous corruption". Eventually he was imprisoned in the Tower of London.

It is perhaps worthy of comment that despite the large number of MPs who were involved in the financial debacle – including some with even closer and more 'profitable' links – it is John Aislabie who is linked in the public perception with the **South Sea Bubble.**

Members expelled from Parliament associated with South Sea Company

23rd Jan 1721 Jacob Sawbridge (Cricklade) Director of the South Sea Company.
28th Jan 1721 Sir Robert Chaplin, Bt. (Great Grimsby) Director of the South Sea Company.
28th Jan 1721 Francis Eyles (Devizes) Director of the South Sea Company.
30th Jan 1721 Sir Theodore Janssen, Bt. (Yarmouth, Isle of Wight) Director of the South Sea Company.
8th Mar 1721 Rt. Hon. John Aislabie (Ripon) Negotiated the agreement to take over the national debt between the South Sea Company and the government, as Chancellor of the Exchequer; received £20,000 of South Sea Company stock; destroyed evidence of his share dealings.
10th Mar 1721 Sir George Caswall (Leominster) Banker of the South Sea Company; obtained for his company £50,000 stock in the South Sea Company while the South Sea Bill was still before Parliament, without paying for it.
8th May 1721 Thomas Vernon (Whitchurch) Attempt to influence a member of the committee on the South Sea bubble in favour of John Aislabie, his brother-in-law.

John Aislabie was subject to several investigations by Parliamentary Committees. One, the Committee of Secrecy of 1719, recorded the change of mind when Aislabie suddenly remembered his gift of shares at below market prices. An extract from the Parliamentary papers of the time gives a strong flavour of the events:

"It is alleged that, in March, 1719, twenty thousand pounds of stock, was bought for John Aislabie, at forty percent below the current market price, by Mr. Wymondeswold and John Falconbridge. In evidence, Falconbridge claims that, after the Committee's preliminary interviews with Wymondeswold, Aislabie had asked to see records of the investigated transactions made in his

name. *When shown these, he, "with Execrations not fit to be repeated, declared, He knew nothing of it... and would swear so in the House, although later he did recall the business. The Committee is pursuing the matter, and orders fifteen individuals relevant to their inquiries to attend the House on Tuesday 28 February. The House resolves that deficiencies in the accounts should be made good by the South Sea Company, and that those concerned in drafting the Bill for the relief of those affected by the business should include clauses to that purpose. Further consideration of the report and new submissions is set for 28 February" (House of Commons. Committee of Secrecy 1719/20).*

After his release from prison, John Aislabie retired to his estate near Ripon and continued the development of the gardens.

John Aislabie died in 1742 aged 71 and both he and his family are commemorated in the memorial in the Cathedral's gallery:

"In the vault beneath are deposited the Right Honourable John Aislabie, dyed 1742, aged 71, of Studley Royal; he married Anne, the daughter of Sr. William Rawlinson, and had issue William, Mary, and Jane; William Aislabie Esquire, dyed 1781, aged 81; the Right Honourable Lady Eliz. Aislabie, daughter of John Earl of Exeter, and wife of William Aislabie, Esquire, dyed 1733, aged 26; also four of their children, John Aislabie dyed 1765, aged 40; William Aislabie dyed 1759, aged 30; Jenny-Maria and Judith who dyed in their Infancy. Elizabeth Aislabie, daughter of Sir Charles Vernon, Knight, and second wife of William Aislabie Esquire, dyed 1780, aged 58; also, their two children Charles Rawlinson and Belinda, who dyed in their Infancy."

Andrew Coulson

The Octagon Tower

Two buildings in John Aislabie's Studley Royal water park

The Banqueting House

Notes and Sources

WALTERS, E.: "Ripon's Prodigal Son", *The Yorkshire Journal,* Winter 1996

Did you know?

The obelisk in Ripon's Market Square, that was provided by John Aislabie in 1702, was the first in England.

Seventeen Feet, Three Wives and at Least a Dozen Children: the Memorial to Sir Edward Blackett

Situated on the southern wall of the south west tower is the impressive, almost voluptuous Baroque memorial to Sir **Edward Blackett,** one of Ripon's wealthiest men in the latter part of the 17th century. Sir Edward Blackett was the son of William Blackett of Newcastle-upon-Tyne, himself a wealthy mining proprietor who in 1673 was created Sir William and the first Baronet Blackett.

Inheriting much of the estate as well as the title in 1680, Edward, second Baronet Blackett of Newcastle, had already been married (to Mary Norton) and been widowed as well as losing his first born son, William, in his infancy.

The next ten years saw Edward re-marry, to another Mary (Yorke), with whom he had twelve children – six boys and six girls – and a fortune which enabled him to establish himself in the neighbourhood of Ripon by purchasing the Newby estate from the Crosland family (see section on Jordan Crosland). Not content with the layout at Newby, he promptly had most of it demolished and rebuilt in its present design in the 1690s. (Celia Fiennes visited Newby on her tour of the north in 1697 and recorded in her diary, 'This was the finest house I saw in Yorkshire'. On Edward Blackett's death, Newby passed to his son and then to his son's nephew, who sold it in 1748 to the Weddell family.

Having already served as Mayor of Newcastle, Edward persuaded Ripon's electorate to vote in sufficient numbers for him so that he was returned in 1689 as Member of Parliament for Ripon. It was a short-lived representation and one that preceded the far more infamous 'dynasty' of Ripon MPs from the Aislabie family. (This latter family served almost continuously for 85 years from 1695 to 1780 – despite the catastrophic links to the infamous South Sea Bubble!)

Sir Edward's parliamentary career was not quite over, since in 1698 he was elected and served for two years as MP for Northumberland. Much time was still given to creating the 'new' Newby Hall, where Edward lived until his death in 1718. The death of his second wife, Mary, in 1699, was followed within a short time by yet another marriage, to Diana Booth.

Edward was around 50 years old when he married Diana, herself a widow, and yet again his wife pre-deceased him when she died in 1713.

Memorials of Ripon Cathedral

Memorial to Sir Edward Blackett
and family in the south west tower

The memorial was originally sited in what used to be the Markenfield Chapel in the north transept, beneath what is now the St Wilfrid's window and moved to its present location in the 20th century.

The monument comprises a representation of a stone altar on which Sir Edward is reclining and around which two of his former wives are placed in mourning clothes. As an exercise in genealogy, the inscription is a confusing family tree:

For those who wish to test their genealogical logic, the inscription from the three panels on this imposing memorial is given below:

Here Lyeth ye Body of Sr / Edward Blacket[sic] of Newby / Bart, Eldest Son to Sir William / Blacket [sic] of Newcastle upon Tine [sic] Bart. He was thrice Married First to Mary only / Child of Thomas Norton, of Langthorne, in the / County of York Esqr. She had Issue only one / Child named William. who Died in his Infanc. / She not Long Surviving. Secondly to Mar /, Daughter of Sr John Yorke, of Richmond, Knigt [sic] / who had Issue Six Sons (viz) William, Edward / John, Thomas, Christopher, and Henry, and / Six Daughter, Elizabeth, Henrietta=Maria, Alethea / Isabella, Ann and Christiana. His third Wife was / Diana Lady Delava, Relict of Sr Ralph Delaval / of Seaton Delaval Bart. Daughter to George / Lord Delamere and Sister to Henry firs [sic] Earl of Warington [sic]. She had Issue by Sr Ralph Delaval / only one Daughter named Diana. Married to / William Eldest Son of Sr Edward Blacket [sic]

Ye said Diana died the / Tenth of January Anno / 1710 Leaving Issue only / one Daughter named / Diana / Diana Lady Blackett / Departed this life the / Seventh day of October / Anno 1713/ The said Sir Edward / Blackett died Apr / ye 22nd 1718 / Aged 69

And the Said / William. Blackett also / departed this life / Twenty Third day of February / Anno 1713 / ye Said Elizabeth / Eldest Daughter / of Sr Edward Blackett / who was Marryd [sic] to / John Wise of Ripon / Esq departed this / life the 22nd of / May 1711

If you have managed to draw following conclusions you have done well.

(1) Edward married Mary Norton; one son William (died in infancy);

(2) Edward married Mary Yorke; sons William, Edward, John, Thomas, Christopher, Henry and daughters Elizabeth, Henrietta-Maria, Alethia, Isabella, Ann and Christiana;

(3) Edward married Diana Booth – who already had a daughter also named Diana from a previous marriage.

Daughter Diana was married to William Blackett, eldest son of Sir Edward by his second wife. William's stepmother therefore appears to have become his mother-in-law!

Andrew Coulson

The Oxley Family

There are a number of memorials both inside and outside the Cathedral to the members of the **Oxley** family and it does not take much time to locate at least one of them. There are stone flags in the south aisle (near the entrance to the Saxon Crypt) memorial plaques on the North wall of the south west tower and large pedestal headstones in the graveyard. Deciphering their relationships, their role in the history of Ripon and how they came to be commemorated here is, however, a more challenging task.

The earliest memorial – a flag in the south aisle – bears the inscription:

Charles Oxley / Alderman of Ripon / Died the Second day of Augt: Anno Dom: 1736 / Aetat. 64 / Near to him lieth Sarah / his wife who died Augt. 28; / 1753, Aged 79 / And Amor & Mary his Son / & Daughter / Ellen Wife of the above / Amor Oxley / died 23d. Novr J1773 / Aged 74 Years

What is not stated is that Charles Oxley, born 5th June 1672, was for many years an elected Alderman of this City and served on two occasions as its Mayor, in 1720 and again in 1736. His profession is likewise omitted, which for a surgeon is surprising, especially one with well recognised public service. Charles – and there are a lot of Charles Oxleys in this particular history – was the grandson of the Rev Charles Oxley and son of Charles Oxley who was the first of the Oxleys to arrive in Ripon. This arrival was to take up the position of Master at the Free Grammar School in Ripon. Living in Skellgate, Charles (school master) and Judith had three children, Charles (again), Judith (again) and Amor.

Charles (b 1672) and his wife Sarah, also commemorated here, themselves had six children, yet another Charles, another Judith, another Amor, another Sarah, a Richard and a Mary. This latest Charles was another surgeon as well as an apothecary, Alderman and Mayor, serving in this latter capacity in 1738. Married to Ellen Casse, he died in 1757 without issue and his sister Judith was left to carry on the family name. She had married Christopher Braithwaite in 1727 but her son Christopher – nephew to the childless 1738 Mayor of Ripon – was destined to inherit his uncle's estate, provided he changed his name to Christopher Oxley; a caveat with which young Christopher (in his mid 20's at the time) was happy to comply. Thus it was a Christopher Braithwaite Oxley who married three times:

Sacred / to the memory of / **CHRISTOPHER OXLEY ESQR.** / who departed this Life the tenth Day of / August, 1803, in the 74th Year of his Age. / He was thrice Married: by his first Wife he / had Issue Frances and Juliana: by his second, / two children who died in their Infancy: and by his third, one Son Charles. / His widow caused this Monument to be erected. / DOROTHY, Relict of the above **CHRISTOPHER OXLEY** departed / this Life March 31st 1820, /Aged 76 years.

and his surviving son – yes, another Charles – was himself twice married. Charles' second wife, Anne Margaret Waddilove, brings the family again into closer relationships with the Cathedral as Anne's father was Robert Darley Waddilove who served as Dean here from 1792 to 1828. Charles and Anne's two children were both boys who died while still young and are commemorated here in the south west tower of the Cathedral.

In the 18th century Charles Oxley inherited the Manor of Rogerthorpe in West Yorkshire, which marks the further increase in wealth for a family who until that time appears to have had a moderate level of property and influence. Eventually the Manor was sold by Edmund Beckwith Oxley in 1891 to Lt Col Ramsden for the sum of £12,000 – at least £1 million at today's prices.

Among the other properties owned by the Oxley family was The Hall in Ripon, a "genteel dwelling house" better known today as Minster House. Bought in 1808, by Charles Oxley, it remained in the family until sold in 1960 to the Dean and Chapter of the Cathedral for use as the principal residence of the Dean of Ripon. A portrait of the Charles who purchased The Hall may be seen today at the Courthouse Museum adjacent to the Cathedral grounds. In the Justices' Retiring Room, there are portraits of many past magistrates including Charles who served as a Justice from 1811 to 1873. He was the first Chairman of Petty Sessions, supervised the Poor Law as first Chairman of the Poor Law Guardians and was a member of the committee responsible for building the Prison in 1816 together with the Courthouse building in 1830.

Among the other Oxley memorials worth noting is the granite gravestone of Admiral Charles Lister Oxley RN (died 1920) who served with distinction in the 1856 – 60 Opium Wars with China. It was during this campaign that whilst only a teenaged midshipman he was mentioned with commendation in dispatches. By 1894 he had progressed to his own command of *HMS Swiftsure* and subsequently to retire as Admiral. The gravestone is a rugged cross atop a truncated cone of dark granite, not dissimilar to the shape of naval buoys. His daughter Dorothy, born in 1890 at Ripon to Charles and Emily (née Kearsley, also interred and commemorated in the graveyard at Ripon), married the 14th Viscount Arbuthnott in 1914 and was honoured with an OBE for her charitable works in 1951.

Emily Oxley's other memorial is located in the South West tower among several others to the family. She and Admiral Charles had seven children, all of whom share

The Oxley family memorial

in the remarkable marble tablet. Each member of the family is present as a sculpted head, all be-winged, and Emily is at the top of the memorial with arms extended in either an embracing or protecting gesture.

The epitaph:

SACRED / TO THE MEMORY OF EMILY, / THE BELOVED WIFE OF / ADMIRAL OXLEY / AND ELDEST DAUGHTER OF ROBERT KEARSLEY, J.P. D.I.., OF HIGHFIELD, IN THIS COUNTY, / WHO DIED JANUARY 19TH 1898, / AGED 41 YEARS. / LEAVING ISSUE 2 SONS AND 5 DAUGHTERS. / ADMIRAL C.L. OXLEY, J.P., / WHO DIED JULY 21ST 1920, AGED 78 YEARS. / VIOLET FREMANTLE. / DIED AUGUST 21ST 1944, AGED 62 YEARS. / COMMANDER C.B. OXLEY, R.N. D.S.C. / DIED JANUARY 11TH 1953 AGED 58 YEARS. / CHARLES OXLEY, DIED MAY 9TH 1959 AGED 79 YEARS. / MARGARET WINIFRED ELIOT. / DIED FEB. 13TH 1969 AGED 85 YEARS. / AGNES OXLEY / DIED FEBRUARY 11TH 1971, / AGED 92 YEARS. / ROSE OXLEY. / DIED JANUARY 14TH 1976, / AGED 90 YEARS./ DOROTHY VISCOUNTESS / OF ARBUTHNOT O.B.E., / DIED JULY 27TH / 1990, AGED 100 YEARS.

Of special note is that at the time of their death, each child's head was added to the memorial, the last being that for Dorothy in 1990. This is believed to be the last memorial to be altered or added to within the Cathedral (with the exception of the Chapel of the Resurrection under the Chapter House).

Commander Christopher Oxley's daughter, Mary Elizabeth Darley Oxley, continued he link to the Arbuthnott family when she subsequently married John Arbuthnott, 16th Viscount.

In commemorating the Jubilee of King George V in 1935, Charles Oxley erected a maypole on the village green of Galphay, nr. Ripon. This is also inscribed as a memorial to Admiral Oxley. Still present is a memorial plaque although the pole has been refurbished/replaced on several occasions.

So in summary, the Oxleys were a Master at the Free Grammar School, Aldermen, Mayors, 17/18th century surgeons, and a land owning family with a penchant for the name Charles. As owners of The Hall (now Minster House) from 1808 to 1959 and as a son-in-law to Dean Robert Waddilove they had very close links to Ripon Cathedral. As Admiral, Charles Lister Oxley served with distinction in the Royal Navy and his son, Commander Christopher Bernard Oxley was a pioneering pilot in the First World War serving with gallantry and heroism.

<u>How Commander Oxley's daughter met her Viscount</u>

One morning in the early 1930s, while tidying up at the tennis court at Arbuthnott, the Lord Arbuthnott of that time found he had lost his signet ring. The court was down by the Bervie so the grass round it was very rough. There were three or four of us there including the present Lord Arbuthnott, then a boy of about ten years old. A reward of a ten-shilling note was offered to the finder, probably the equivalent of about £30 today.

For quite two hours we searched on a hot summer morning, feeling that it was like looking for a needle in a haystack. Suddenly there appeared on the scene a small girl, Mary Oxley, the present Lady Arbuthnott, who was staying with her Aunt (her Aunt was Rose Oxley, commemorated on the Oxley family memorial in the Tower) at Parkside Cottage. "What are you doing?" she said. "Looking for a ring," we replied, rather irritably. We were hot and tired. Mary stooped down.

"Is this it?" she asked, holding up a round gold object.

Quite unbelievably, she had walked right on to it. Rather embarrassed, Lord Arbuthnott handed her the ten-shilling note, and I can still see the rueful smile on the face of the boy. Mary however returned from where she had come, not only with her fortuitous gains, but also having had what may well have been her first sighting of her future husband.

(From: A Reminiscence by Mrs Blair-Imrie, Little Pleasance, Edzell:

http://www.scottishcorpus.ac.uk/corpus/search/document.php?documentid=1376)

Andrew Coulson

Notes and Sources

National Archives, Kew, "Will of Christopher Oxley", 1804

The memoir retold in the box above and the war story recounted on the next page help bring two members of the Oxley family into sharper focus.

Distinguished Service

Commander Christopher Bernard Oxley, RN, was awarded his Distinguished Service Cross in 1916 for his actions during the early days of the Royal Naval Air Service. The citation understates it as awarded for: "Acting as Observer with Flight Lieutenant Edward H Dunning DSC as Pilot, on an escort and reconnaissance patrol for a flight of bombing machines on the Bulgarian Coast on 20 June 1916. Two enemy machines were engaged at close range and forced to retire".

In reality, the 21 year old Oxley was part of a two man crew of a Sopwith fighter plane and in addition to deterring the two enemy fighters, he provided a tourniquet to his injured pilot and then climbed in mid air out of his rear seat into the pilot seat to fly the plane successfully back to base – despite extensive damage to the fuselage and fuel tank. His injured pilot spent the return trip

maintaining pressure on his leg tourniquet and also via his thumbs on holes in the fuel tank so that they would have enough fuel to complete their return flight.

(Of interest is that the pilot whose life Christopher Oxley undoubtedly saved went on to become Squadron Leader Dunning and he was the first man to ever land a plane – a Sopwith Pup - successfully on a ship – HMS Furious - at sea. Launching planes had been relatively straightforward, but the large differences in speed of plane v ship made it a perilous task in 1917. As it was, Dunning lost his life one week after his first successful landing when he tried to repeat his feat and plunged overboard).

www.1914-1918.invisionzone.com

A Sopwith Pup

The Dilessi Murders:
the Death of Frederick Grantham Vyner

The two most easterly windows in the North choir aisle are dedicated to the memory of members of the Vyner family. That dedicated to **Frederick Grantham Vyner** comprises four panels of biblical scenes: Abraham and Isaac, the anointing of David, the stoning of Stephen and the raising of Lazarus. As well as having considerable artistic merit, this window recalls a 19th century tragedy for the Vyner family.

On 11th April 1870, Lord and Lady Muncaster and their friend Frederick Vyner, on holiday in Athens, decided to visit Marathon with a secretary at the British Legation, E. H. C. Herbert (the first cousin of the Earl of Caernarvon), a resident Englishman (Edward Lloyd) with his wife and young daughter, and a friend from the Italian Legation (Count Alberto de Boyl). Although careful arrangements were made with the police to ensure the safety of the party, they were captured by what would now be called terrorists in the Greek countryside, while touring the area near the village of Dilessi, around Marathon.

The two ladies and the young girl were released with demands for a large ransom of £32,000 and a 'safe passage', set by the kidnappers for the release of the group. The Greek government were, however, constitutionally bound to 'never grant amnesty' to members of these gangs – of which there were several, all supporting different political or criminal goals.

Frederick Grantham Vyner, from Newby Hall, was then aged 23 and a student at Christchurch, Oxford. The negotiations with the kidnappers were badly handled, with the Greek Government, British Embassy and other bands of brigands all having some part in the dealings. Eventually it was agreed to pay the ransom demanded, but no amnesty would be granted.

Although he was chosen by the kidnap gang to be freed as a messenger between the bandits and the Government, Frederick Vyner preferred to let one of his fellow hostages go, Lord Muncaster, as he was a married man. Muncaster left the camp promising to return but never did so.

Frederick was shot as the kidnappers executed their remaining hostages and in the ensuing fight, the soldiers, sent to free them, allowed half of the gang to escape. The last written words from Frederick Vyner – in a note sent while held by the

Section from the window commemorating the murdered Frederick Grantham Vyner

kidnappers - are inscribed in a memorial in York Minster: *"We must trust to God that we may die bravely as Englishmen should do"*.

Frederick's body was taken to Gautby, in Lincolnshire, to the Vyner family Church and lies there below the altar.

As a consequence of the debacle, the Greek government paid compensation and this money was used to build two Churches near Ripon in his memory. They are the Church of Christ the Consoler at Skelton-on-Ure and the Church of St Mary at Studley. Frederick Vyner's mother commissioned the window here in the Cathedral and also the east window in the Latin Chapel of Oxford Cathedral in his memory - beautiful memorials to a much-loved young man, whose chivalry cost him dearly.

Andrew Coulson

Notes and Sources

JENKINS, Romily: *The Dilessi Murders, (1961)*

William Weddell (1736–92)

The bust of William Weddell contained within the classical half-rotunda memorial in the south transept is in fact one of a small set of marble busts created by Joseph Nollekens. Weddell was a keen neo-classicist and the Grecian style of his monument reflects this.

Mrs Weddell's inscription is a marvellous tribute to her husband:

To the memory of William Weddell, Esq., of Newby,
in whom every virtue that ennobles the mind
as united with every elegance that adorns it.
This monument, a faint emblem of his refined
taste, is dedicated by his widow.
Whom what awaits while yet she strays
Along the lonely vale of days,
A pang, to secret sorrow dear,
A sigh, an unavailing tear,
Till time shall every grieve remove
With life with memory, and with love.

Note that there are no dates included in this epitaph. Perhaps this is to reinforce the symbol of eternity represented by the snake with its tail in its mouth which can be seen on the plinth.

There are several occasions when the history of Newby Hall joins that of Ripon Cathedral and the memorial to William Weddell is one of those points of convergence. Newby Hall was occupied by Jordan Crosland [see chapter on Crosland] until the 1690s when he sold it to Sir Edward Blackett – also commemorated in the Cathedral – who was the gentleman who demolished the original house and built the property seen today as Newby Hall.

In 1748, Blackett's great-nephew sold the estate to William Weddell, who must have been a man of great taste and knowledge, and indeed was a prominent member of the Dilettanti Society. He made the Grand Tour in 1765-6 and soon after his return to England made contact with most of the leading neo-classical architects, including of course Robert Adam.

Weddell's intention was to refurbish the house for his classical sculpture (he

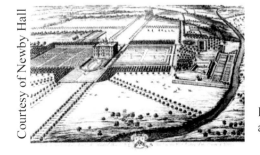

Drawing for Sir Edward Blackett of Newby Hall and Gardens by Kip, mid 18th century

Courtesy of Newby Hall

65

imported nineteen chests of classical sculpture from Rome) and for the set of Gobelin tapestries he had ordered while abroad in 1766.

John Carr probably added the two wings to the east of the house and remodelled much of the main block at this time, turning the house around and rebuilding the three central bays of the east elevation. If Carr planned the Statue Gallery in its original form it was not to Weddell's entire satisfaction because Robert Adam was commissioned in 1767 to complete the galleries and to decorate the Tapestry Room and some of the interior of the house.

Courtesy of Newby Hall

Batoni portrait of William Weddell

One of Weddell's greatest acquisitions was the famous Barberini Venus, which was held at Newby Hall from 1765 until 2002 when it was sold to a middle-eastern magnate for £8 million.

Weddell died in 1792 without children and Newby passed to his cousin, Thomas Philip Robinson, who changed his name to Weddell, although he had already succeeded his father and become the 3rd Lord Grantham. An amateur architect himself (he later became the first President of the RIBA), much of the design of the so-called Regency Dining Room is attributable to him.

Elizabeth Weddell (1749 –1831)

Elizabeth, widow of William, erected the memorial to her husband, but is not herself commemorated on the monument. She survived a further 39 years after William's early death and died at 6, Upper Brook Street Mayfair, London in 1831. She directed in her Will her desire to be buried at Ripon "with minimal expense".

<u>**Did you know?**</u>

From about 1660 until the arrival of mass rail transit in the 1820s the **Grand Tour** was a "gap-year experience" for wealthy young Englishmen to round-off their education.

A typical Grand Tour included France, in particular Paris, Switzerland and Italy, focussing focusing on Florence, Venice and Rome to study the classical ruins. A visit to the recently discovered archaeological sites of Herculaneum and Pompeii, with perhaps an ascent of Mount Vesuvius, would have been a highlight. The return journey often included the German speaking countries as well.

As well as meeting fashionable society in other countries, these journeys proved useful for collecting works of art and archaeological artefacts.

The **Society of Dilettanti** was a club of gentlemen which sponsored the study of Classical art and the creation of new work in the style. It was founded as a London dining club in 1734 by men who had been on the Grand Tour.

Andrew Coulson

Notes and Sources

Newby Hall and gardens are open to the public. For further information see:

http://www.newbyhall.com

The sculptor: Joseph Nollekens (1737 - 1823) Joseph Nollekens was a famous portrait sculptor and member of the Royal Academy. He enjoyed the patronage of George III and was commissioned to create a number of Church monuments for fashionable society.

The Barberini Venus: Having bought the Barberini Venus (named after the collection it once was part of) Weddell returned to Newby in the summer of 1765 and commissioned a suitable gallery for the sculptures and other antiquities he had purchased in Rome. The re-named Weddell Venus received a prominent niche decorated with refined Neo-classical plasterwork.

In 2002 it broke the world auction record for an antiquity after selling for almost £8 million. A laser-made Carrara marble copy replaces the original at Newby whilst the original is in the ownership of Sheikh Saud-al-Thoni of Qatar.

Memorials with an

American Connection

Edmund Jenings (1731-1819)

The memorial to Edmund Jenings is on the wall in the Chapel of the Holy Spirit. It is a polished white marble tablet with raised inscription panel, having *patee formee* brackets (top and bottom parts of a cross which is wider at the outer ends than in the centre) at the head and foot. The inscription is incised, black painted Roman capitals.

Courtesy of Virginia Historical Society

Edmund Jenings, framed miniature
by unknown artist

The Edmund Jenings commemorated here was born in Annapolis, Maryland in 1731 but spent much of his life in England. He was one of a succession of Edmunds in the Jenings family (see family tree below), a family closely involved as Britain's young American colony determined its independence.

Three generations earlier, Edmund's great grandfather, Sir Edmund Jenings, was MP for Ripon. Sir Edmund's second son went to Virginia as a young man and became the first of the family to live in 'the Colonies'. Eventually, he owned a tobacco plantation and had named his fine house Rippon Hall and he had held office as

Attorney General for Virginia. Before he died, he had had to sell Rippon Hall to pay off his debts.

His son, another Edmund, was Secretary of State for Maryland before retiring to Bath in England. As a young man, he married Anna Vanderheyen and our Edmund Jenings was born. He went to England as a young boy, was educated at Eton and Cambridge and he studied law before being called to the bar.

Virginia Historical Society

Cranstone painting of
Rippon Hall. Virginia

Because of his ancestors' marriages and business interests Edmund had access to the best families in Virginia. He was a friend and patron of the young American portrait artist Charles Willson Peale. While Peale was in London getting help and advice from another American artist, Jenings commissioned him to paint William Pitt, Earl of Chatham, in appreciation for Chatham's opposition to the Stamp Act. This painting still hangs in the Maryland State House.

Our Edmund was one of a group of expatriate Americans who were advocates of American rights during the Revolution. He spent time in Paris, probably as a secret agent, and also at the Court of Brussels where he corresponded with Benjamin Franklin and John Adams. While in Brussels, Jenings received a miniature portrait of George Washington from his artist friend Peale. There are copies of letters written by him in the Maryland Archives and also a letter in the Adams papers in which he admits to writing an 'anonymous' pamphlet in 1778. This pamphlet, *Considerations on the mode and terms of a treaty of peace with America*, proposed that Great Britain acknowledge the independence of America.

As a result, his property in Maryland was not confiscated and this meant he continued to have a small but independent income. Edmund Jenings kept active in his old age, visited the Kensington Library daily and was said to have "agreeable manners". He did not appear to have any property remaining in Ripon as he is purported to have sold his estate here in 1758.

Edmund Jenings and his widow Elizabeth are buried in Kensington Churchyard. The memorial to Elizabeth and their son Charles is nearby that of Edmund Jenings in the Chapel of the Holy Spirit. This is a wall tablet which is ornate, being a polished black marble slab on which is superimposed a white marble tablet with stepped cornice above a row of five rosettes. The inscription panel, in incised black painted Roman capitals, is flanked by decorated panels and a decorated bottom panel.

The connection to the nearby memorial to Robert Porteus is that Edmund's aunt Elizabeth Jenings was Robert Porteus's second wife. Edmund's other aunt, Frances, married Charles Grymes and they were great grandparents of General Robert E. Lee, of the Confederate army in the American civil war. Edmund's sister, Ariana, was the mother of Edmund Jenings Randolph, who became the first Attorney General of the United States.

The Epitaph of Edmund Jenings:

To the memory of **EDMUND JENINGS**
Formerly of this place, and of the Middle Temple,
London, Esquire, who was born in Anapolis,
In the British Province of Maryland
In the month of August 1731
And died at Kensington in the county of Middlesex'
On 29th July 1819, aged nearly 88 years.
His widow and only surviving child,
Grateful for his conjugal and parental tenderness,
Erect this marble.

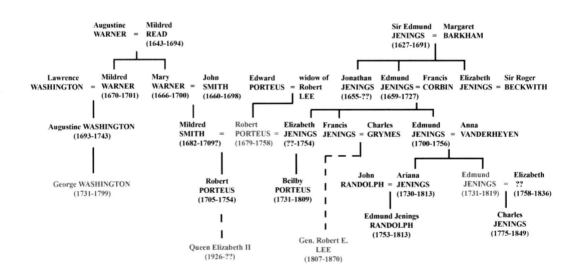

Family tree linking Edmund Jenings and Robert Porteus

Notes and Sources

Ripon Millenary

Information from Cathy Hellier, Williamsburg from Colonial Williamsburg Foundation

Virginia Historical Society 1947 Vol 55

Peale in London   www.lewis-clark.org

Annapolis Complex Collection

Archives of Maryland Online Vol 43, p 477,478

US Senate Art and History George Washington at Princeton

www.reesco.com catalogue 255 section v 113

Records of Antebellum Southern Plantations www.lexisnexis.com/academic/guides/Ash/plan1302.pdf Series M

Did you know?

The flag of the United States is said to be based on the Coat of Arms of the Washington family. This Coat of Arms, seen on the Norton window on the north wall of the nave, has the red mullets (spiked discs on a spur) on a white background changed into white stars on a blue background.

A committee, one of whom was Colonel George Washington, discussed the design for the flag and the first flag was made by Betsy Ross after suggestions she had made about the design.

Detail from the Norton (Grantley) window in Ripon Cathedral showing the Washington Coat of Arms

Robert Porteus (1679-1758)

The memorial to Robert Porteus is on the wall of the Chapel of the Holy Spirit. It is a rectangular slate slab on which is superimposed a rectangular polished white marble inscription tablet.

The Robert Porteus commemorated here was the son of Edward Porteus who emigrated to Virginia from Scotland. In 1693, Edward was recommended to the Council (His Majesty's Council or Upper House of Legislature), having been vestryman of Petsworth Parish since 1681. His son Robert was also vestryman in 1704 as well as a Council member. In 1700, Robert married Mildred Smith and they are reputed to have had many children.

By 1720, the small landed aristocracy in Virginia experienced a vast increase in the number of new settlers and three times as many blacks as at the beginning of the century. Small farmers and planters interfered with the patriarchal pattern in which Robert had been brought up. At this time it was the habit of southern settlers to cling to their Englishness and send their children back to England to be educated. This may be why he decided to emigrate to England - so that his children could have "better instruction" at English schools. He moved first to York and then to Ripon.

Robert Porteus married twice. His son Robert, by his first marriage, was a minister in the Church and it is through his line that Queen Elizabeth II is descended. George Washington was a relative of his first wife, Mildred. Robert's second marriage was to Elizabeth Jenings, aunt of the Edmund Jenings also commemorated in Ripon Cathedral. They had a son, Beilby, who became Bishop of Chester and then Bishop of London.

Robert became steward of Brafferton Manor, near Helperby. This manor had been purchased in 1694 with a bequest from Sir Robert Boyle, the distinguished philosopher, who left the residue of his estate "for propagation of Christian religion among infidels". The estate proceeds were sent to Virginia to fund "The Brafferton", a building in William and Mary College in Williamsburg, for the education of "Indian children" (native American children).

When in America, Robert Porteus had made his money from tobacco plantations and presumably this helped finance him in England. In his will, Robert Porteus did "give to my poor slave Peter now in Virginia his freedom from slavery and that a comfortable maintenance be provided for him, including a coat, waistcoat and breeches, two canvas shirts, two pairs of yarn stockings and two pairs of shoes be provided every year so long as he lives".

Brafferton Hall, Williamsburg, Virginia

There are connections to Brafferton Manor in the memorials in the Cathedral. Jordan Crosland, whose memorial is in the south transept and is referred to elsewhere in this book, bought the lease for the manor in March 1664-5 for about two years.

In the North aisle, there is a slate flagstone commemorating **William Hinde**, who had been been employed by Robert Porteus as a lawyer and had replaced Robert as steward of Brafferton Manor before the position was given to Robert's son-in-law, Edward Thomson. There is no record that Hinde had been to Virginia, but there is correspondence from Beilby relating to Hinde's stewardship of the manor. In a letter to John Blair re Brafferton Estate, Porteus is critical of Hinde's management of the estate: ..."that Mr Hind is a most improper man to have the management of the Estate...an artful, self-interested, litigious attorney..." His motivation for casting aspersions on Hinde's character may have something to do with the fact that Porteus wanted his son-in-law, Edward Thompson, to be given the stewardship of the Brafferton Estate. Whilst this position was remunerated with only £20 per annum, it appears it afforded considerable opportunities for perks!

It is interesting that Robert's Anglican reformer son Beilby was an early slave abolitionist. After America's Declaration of Independence and death of his father, Beilby was able to divert the Brafferton Manor funds away from the education of native American children. Instead, they went to help with the education of slaves in the British West India Islands.

Ripon Grammar School has a Porteus house commemorating their one-time pupil, Beilby Porteus, and there is a memorial window to him in the library of Ripon Cathedral.

The Epitaph of Robert Porteus:

Near this place
Are deposited the Remains
of ROBERT PORTEUS ESQ.
A native of Virginia and a member of his Majesty's Council
Or Upper House of Legislature in that Province
From thence he removed to England
And resided first at York Afterwards in this Town
Where he died August 8[th.] 1738
Aged 79 years

Moira Stalker

Notes and Sources

We thank Francis Redpath concerning information on Beilby Porteus

William and Mary Quarterly History Magazine vol 3 no1 (July 1984)

The Smiths of Virginia William and Mary Quarterly vol 4 no 1

The Queen's American ancestors: www.bigballoonmusic.com/goddardreagan/The Queen'sAmericanAncestors.htm

Information from Cathy Hellier, Colonial Williamsburg Foundation

www.genuki.org

Brafferton Parish information from Bulmer, 1890

www.brycchancarey.com/abolition/porteus.htm

Wm and Mary Quarterly from the Dawson papers, Library of Congress.

Ripon and the British Empire

Among recent generations, to talk of Empire, in a British context, is to bring to mind the largest Empire the world has ever seen (in population and size) – a far-flung group of multi-ethnic territories in many varied climes associated (especially) with the later years of Queen Victoria's reign and the first part of the 20th Century.

Everyone in Britain was influenced by the Empire in many and varied ways; even something as prosaic as the great British institution of the "cuppa tea" – which has been readily available to all for several generations, but in the 18th century, was an aristocratic/gentry preserve. On a broader canvas, within large sections of the general population there was a pride that so much of the world map was coloured red – showing parts of the British Empire. This was due to vigorous colonisation/ annexation policies supported by the Royal Navy, which controlled the shipping lanes, and the scatter of army units throughout the Empire - often local troops with British officers.

As we will see, Ripon sent representatives to some of these far-away places to take part in empire building, whether military, naval or economic or even as part of a team of explorers. Some of these men never returned. Their memorials remind us of a price we do not often take into account when looking at the red bits on a map, the lives of these young men. Several memorials stand out as representative of the "Imperial" phase of British History which began in the 17th century and – despite the set-back of the thirteen American colonies gaining independence - continued to a high point in the late 19th/early 20th century.

Soldiers

The easternmost memorial, made of brass, in the north nave aisle commemorates several members of the **Bruce** family. One was an army surgeon who served in the Peninsular War and was, then, at Waterloo; another was a senior judge in Jamaica; yet another was a captain in the Royal Navy and died while in command of his ship HMS *Galatea* while on escort duty at Queen Victoria's funeral. One can only speculate how the rest of the crew reacted to their Captain's death at such an historic moment! A fourth member of the Bruce family was an officer in the 8th (King's) Regiment and served in the Crimea. The 8th Foot's main recruiting area was in Liverpool and later was known as the King's (Liverpool) Regiment.

Co-incidentally, some 60 years later, a future Dean (Frederick Llewelyn Hughes) was also an officer in that regiment, in the early years of the first World War. He was Dean from 1951 to 1967. The Cathedral forecourt was relaid in his memory in 1970, which is mentioned on a plaque near the forecourt, and his simple memorial plaque is in the Chapel of the Resurrection.

The north west corner of the north transept could be called the Staveley corner as the two windows in the angle are both family memorials and the stone memorial alongside the north door is to General **Miles Staveley**. The descendent of a prominent local family, he is the namesake of his ancestor Miles Staveley who lived at Rippone Parke in the 16th century. The family,

Mary and the child Jesus:
the statue, one of three
by Harold Gosney, was donated
in memory of Simon Staveley

represented by Robert Arthur Miles Staveley of North Stainley Hall, is still found in our area today. One of the three Gosney statues in Ripon Cathedral, namely the one with Mary and the child Jesus dancing, was given in memory of **Simon Staveley,** his brother (1949-1998).

Our Miles obtained a cornetcy in the Royal Horse Guards, in January 1759 and served with that regiment for a period of forty years. His first essay in arms was during the Seven Years' War in Germany, where he served under Prince Ferdinand of Brunswick.

He was promoted to the rank of Lieutenant Colonel in 1794 and in 1798 to that of major general. In 1799 he obtained the Colonelcy of the 28th or the Duke of York's own Regiment of Light Dragoons, which was disbanded at the peace of Amiens in 1802. In the following year he obtained the command of the Royal Irish Dragoon Guards and was subsequently promoted to the rank of Lieutenant General. He died aged 77 in 1814.

Did you know?

Miles Staveley's distinguished military career included an event made famous in a nursery rhyme. In 1793 he served in Flanders with Frederick, Duke of York. "Grand" the Duke may well have been – but at 30 years of age could he be classed as "old", and in the (at most) gently undulating country of coastal Flanders, where was "the hill" that the 10,000 men marched up and down?

> **"Oh, the Grand Old Duke of York**
> **He had 10,000 men**
> **He marched them up to the top of the hill**
> **And marched them down again..."**

Nonetheless, Miles, as a Major in the Royal Horse Guards, would have ridden up the hill anyway, - even if this most famous of British Army manoeuvres ever took place!?!

Also in the North Transept are the memorials to the **Waddilove** brothers and grandsons of Dean Waddilove. One reads like a very critical newspaper report while the other is more matter of fact.

The first inscription reads:

SACRED TO THE MEMORY OF
LIEUTENANT FRANCIS WILLIAM WADDILOVE OF H.M. 53RD REGT.
(SECOND SURVIVING SON THE REVD. W.J.D. WADDILOVE)
WHO FELL THE VICTIM OF A LONG MARCH, ABOUT 250 MILES, FROM LAHORE TO
RAWUL - PINDEE IN THE PUNJAUB DURING THE VERY HOTTEST PERIOD
OF A SEASON UNUSUAL EVEN IN THE INDIAN CLIMATE;
WHEN ACCORDING TO THE REGISTER KEPT IN THE SURVEYOR GENERAL'S
OFFICE, THE HEAT EXCEEDED 100 DEGREES OF FAHRENHT.
DAILY AT NOON IN THE SHADE.
ON THE 20TH. OF APRIL THE ORDERS WERE FOR "THE DEPOT" TO REMAIN
AT LAHORE TILL THE HEATS WERE OVER, BUT ON THE 27TH. THESE ORDERS
WERE SUDDENLY SUPERSEDED BY AN ORDER TO MARCH, AND ON THE 7TH.
OF MAY THE 3 COMPANIES LEFT LAHORE, LIEUT. W. HAVING
CHARGE OF COMP. No. 4.
AFTER SEVERE SUFFERING BOTH BY MEN AND OFFICERS,
THE SURVIVORS REACHED THEIR DESTINATION ABOUT THE 28TH OF MAY,
AS ON THE 29TH. HE WAS "IN ORDERS" FOR 6 MONTHS SICK LEAVE
TO THE NORTHERN HILLS", IT WAS HOWEVER TOO LATE, AND
ON THE 4TH. OF JUNE 1849 HE DIED OF THE FEVER THUS PRODUCED,
AGED 25 YEARS AND ELEVEN MONTHS,
AND HIS REMAINS SLEEP IN THE PLAINS OF RAWUL-PINDEE,
HAVING SERVED H.M. IN IRELAND, CANADA, NOVA, (sic) SCOTIA,
AND WEST AND EAST INDIES 7 YEARS.
HIS SORROWING PARENTS ERECT THIS TABLET IN REMEMBRANCE
OF A BELOVED AND DESERVEDLY LAMENTED CHILD
IN THE CATHEDRAL OF HIS NATIVE PLACE, AND IN MEMORY OF
THE MANY WHO PERISHED WITH HIM ON THIS FATAL MARCH.
AUGUST 31ST , 1849.

An administrative error of gigantic proportions! One can only guess at the feelings of those associated with this totally unnecessary loss of life, not only of Francis William Waddilove, but also of many of his comrades.

A fitting memorial to a soldier is the second stained glass window from the east in the south nave aisle. It could be called the Knight's window as it depicts an idealised view of medieval knighthood and features two Old Testament military

The window memorial to William Slayter Smith, showing the Archangel Michael with Joshua and David from the Old Testament

heroes, Joshua and David and the Archangel Michael, general of the heavenly host. The brass dedication below the window reads:

IN MEMORY OF WILLIAM SLAYTER SMITH, OF GREEN ROYD, RIPON, WHO DIED 18TH JULY 1865 AGED 72 YEARS: CAPTAIN AND ADJUTANT OF THE YORKSHIRE REGIMENT OF HUSSAR YEOMANRY FROM 1822 TO 1864: HE SERVED AS LIEUTENANT IN THE 13TH LIGHT DRAGOONS IN THE PENINSULAR WAR IN THE CAMPAIGNS OF 1810, 1811 AND 1812, AND WAS ONCE SEVERELY, AND TWICE SLIGHTLY WOUNDED. HE ALSO SERVED IN THE 10TH HUSSARS AT THE BATTLE OF WATERLOO.

Soldier and Sailor: Memorial plaques to the Waddilove brothers, Lt. Francis William and Lt. Robert James Darley R.N., whose tragic epitaphs are shown in full in this chapter

Sailors

The brother of the unfortunate victim of the Rawalpindi march, **Robert Darley Waddilove**, was a naval officer and was buried at sea in the Pacific.

WHICH HOPE WE HAVE AS AN ANCHOR OF THE SOUL

BOTH SURE AND STEADFAST HEBREWS VI. 19.

SACRED TO THE MEMORY OF

LIEUT. ROBERT JAMES DARLEY WADDILOVE R.N. OF H.M.S. AMERICA,

WHO DIED AT SEA OCTR. 7TH. 1844 WITHIN A FEW DAYS SAIL OF VALPARAISO.

HIS REMAINS ARE COMMITTED TO THE DEPTHS OF THE SOUTH PACIFIC,

TILL THAT GREAT DAY WHEN EARTH AND SEA SHALL GIVE UP THEIR DEAD.

AGED 25 YEARS, 13 OF WHICH WERE SPENT IN H.M. SERVICE.

HE WAS BORN AT THORP MAY 12TH. 1819.

THE ELDEST GRANDSON OF THE VERY REVD. R. D. WADDILOVE D.D.

MANY YEARS DEAN OF THIS CHURCH.

THIS SLAB IS DEDICATED TO HIS MEMORY

BY HIS AFFLICTED PARENTS, APRIL 1ST 1845.

Courtesy of Southold Historical Society

HMS *Sylph* by B. J. Phillips

At that time, the Royal Navy's main function was to maintain the Pax Britannica (a deliberate copying of the Roman ideal). This was done through a series of naval stations around the globe supplying the needs of numerous gunboats. Interestingly, when Robert Darley Waddilove died, Valparaiso was used by the Royal Navy by arrangement with the newly independent Chilean Government and was the only R.N. station, at that time, on soil not claimed to be part of the British Empire. Later Valparaiso was superseded as the main

Beautiful window memorial to
Lt. Constantine Browne, R.N.
He died in 1815 when HMS *Sylph*
grounded and broke up in heavy
weather off Long Island, New York

R.N. station in the Eastern Pacific by Esquimault, on Vancouver Island – which was rapidly built up during the early 1850s to forestall any Russian activity in the North Pacific during the Crimean War. In those days, Alaska was part of the Russian Empire.

The window above the Waddilove memorials records that two members of the Browne family were Naval officers. Lt. **Constantine Browne** died in particularly tragic circumstances when he was drowned in 1814 while serving on HMS *Sylph* (see picture on page 80). The *Sylph*, a Bermuda-built sloop of war (rated as an 18 gunner) was very active off the New England coast, and especially in Long Island Sound, during the War of 1812 between America and Britain. This included, in June 1814, the destruction of an American Torpedo Boat - a very early form of submarine, though only semi-submersible.

In January 1815, during a severe gale which included heavy snow, the *Sylph* struck Southampton Bar at the east end of Long Island and broke in two. Only six of the 117 crew survived and these were taken to New York as prisoners-of-war. An eyewitness account of the event records: "When the ship came on shore all sail was standing and the deck covered with sailors. In an instant all the masts went by the boards, at that time, yes in an instant more than one Hundred men went from this world to eternity. They appeared indifferent about their own safety they would assist one another though in equal danger, but soon they were all drownded (*sic*) or dashed to pieces." (H.T. Dering in a letter to his sister). Some spectators of this tragic sinking helped the six survivors. The British naval commander, Admiral Hotham, got a message through to the local US citizens thanking them for their humane treatment of the survivors.

HM navy was not the only career option for adventurous and sea-loving youngsters. Then as now, joining the merchant marine was a possibility and one lucky boy with a Ripon connection got to sign on as a midshipman on a voyage of exploration.

Explorers

Prominent amongst Ripon's monuments is that to Commander **John Elliott,** RN (1759 -1834) (south aisle, baptistery), who was a member of Captain James Cook's second world voyage 1772-5. Elliott wrote an account of his Cook expedition, undertaken when he was about thirteen, and later continued it to give details of his naval life

Holmefield House, Ripon (pictured in 2008)
was once Elliott House,
home of Cmdr. John Elliott

including eleven battles. He was wounded twice, at the Battle of the Sts, Jamaica in 1782. He retired to Ripon, building Elliott House (still standing as Holmefield), never having achieved the captaincy of a warship which he craved. Elliott was much praised by his superiors – at least, he tells us so – and was particularly skilled in mapping and navigation. To be 'cool, firm and collected' was his ideal, and as a water-drinker, one feels sure that on board he was such, despite the duels he fought and his family squabbles.

Elliott's monument, by Robert Whitton of Ripon, is in the Gothic revival style, with family heraldry at the top and a long interesting inscription which records deaths of many of his children. Elliott's will requested 'a neat marble monument'. It was put up by John Bardoe Elliott (born 1785, died at Patna 1863), John's eldest son, an Indian magistrate and administrator - and here we are, like his father, in the Empire, for he was sent out to India to make his fortune, and quickly rose in the civil service.

John Elliott himself had worked for the East India Company between his Cook trip and rejoining the Royal Navy, but he had not found great fortune.

John Elliott's other surviving son, (Sir) **William Henry Elliott** (1792-1874) had a very distinguished career, joining the 51st King's Own Light Infantry as ensign in 1809, and serving in the Peninsular War, and at Waterloo, of which he provided his father with a few sketches for *his* life story. William Henry was made general in 1871 and was full of honours, having served in many quarters of the world. His main achievement was the saving of the Rangoon community in the 1850s during the Burmese War. Like his father, William Henry twice suffered injuries in service to his country.

Neither John Bardoe nor William Henry Elliott has monuments in Ripon Cathedral, though many of their family are shown on the main monument.

The other Elliott monument below John's is that of **Neville Bowes Elliott-Cooper** (1889-1918), whose illustrious army service was recognized by the awards of DSO, MC and VC (see World War I memorials).

Bishops

Whilst much wealth in England was based on the slave trade and income from plantations, some subjects of the British Empire began to question the morality of the institution of slavery. A fierce campaign over many years was waged to abolish slavery. Initially, only the trade in slaves was forbidden (British Parliamentary Act of 1807), but this was followed in 1833 by the abolition of slavery throughout the Empire. One of the early proponents of the anti-slavery movement in Britain was **Beilby Porteus,** a Bishop with considerable Riponian connections. He was the son of Robert Porteus (see the chapter on the American Connection) and his coat of arms, as Bishop of London, can be seen in the Library East Window (see Heraldry chapter).

In 1783, some four years before the establishment of the Society for the Abolition of the Slave Trade and while he was Bishop of Chester, Beilby Porteus preached a sermon in which he suggested that the most deserving slaves might be allowed to "work out their freedom by degrees" and should be given sufficient education to understand the Christian message. With the hindsight of well over two centuries this seems a relatively mild concession, and appears to assume that the freed slaves would be replaced by other slaves coming in! It is nonetheless important as one of the earliest hints of disquiet in the established Church of England.

It is somewhat ironic that the Porteus family had connections with Virginia, where his family had owned an estate worked by slaves, and which, eighty years after his sermon, was a key part of the Confederacy (of slave owning states) in the American Civil War; indeed Richmond was not only the state capital but was also the Confederate Capital. Even more poignant was the occasion of the delivery of the 1783 sermon. It was the annual meeting of the Society for the Propagation of the Gospel in Foreign Parts. The Society owned the Codrington Estate in Barbados, which was worked by slaves and had the reputation of being notoriously mis-managed!

Politicians

In addition to soldiers and sailors, Ripon also provided politicians for the administration of the Empire. Following the re-organisation of the Government of India after the Indian Mutiny (1856), one of the most important, high-profile political figures in the Empire was the Viceroy of India. From 1880-1885 the Viceroy was **George Frederick Robinson**, the owner of Studley Royal and the 1st Marquess of Ripon. Though there are memorials to some of his relatives in the Cathedral (see the section on The Dilessi Murders - Frederick Grantham Vyner), he and the marchioness have a magnificent tomb in St Mary's, Studley Royal. There is also a memorial to him in St Wilfred's R.C. Church in Ripon and his statue is in the Spa Gardens. His arms can be seen in two of the north choir aisle windows (see chapter on heraldry).

Control of trade in all kinds of commodities coupled with large investments in the Empire – and other parts of the world such as South America – also contributed to Britain's dominant position in Victorian times. Indeed, it has often been said that "trade followed the flag"; though the relationship between economic and political expansion appears quite complex sometimes. The importance of "Merchant (Ad) venturer" companies, such as the Hudson Bay Co. (founded 1670) and the East India Co. (founded 1599), in the expansion of the Empire is considerable.

Unfortunately, Ripon is more associated with a similar company – the South Sea Company – which collapsed spectacularly in 1720 – The South Sea Bubble" – triggering a severe financial crisis. For his part in this, **John Aislabie** (then Chancellor of the Exchequer in Walpole's government) was imprisoned in the Tower and only let out after paying a hefty fine and being barred from public office for life (see section on John Aislabie in the chapter on the Good and the Sometimes Not So Good)). While his memorial is in the Cathedral on the gallery outside the library, his greatest "memorial" is the early 18th century water garden at Studley Royal.

Derek Ching

Notes and Sources

We thank the Southold Historical Society, USA, for information on HMS *Sylph*.

The section on John Elliott is by David Lee.

The John Elliott manuscript account of his life including the Cook journey is in the British Library, photocopy in Ripon Library, and is partly published in John Elliott and Richard Pickersgill: *Captain Cook's second voyage*, edited by Christine Holmes (1984).

W.H. Elliott's life is included in both the old and newer versions of the *Dictionary of National Biography*.

For the Church's relations with the pro- and anti- slavery movements and the role of Beilby Porteus see:

BARCLAY, John MG: *"Am I not a Man and a Brother?" The Bible and the British Anti-Slavery Campaign*. In: *Expository Times*, vol 119, October 2007.

For material on Valparaiso see:

DALZIEL, Nigel: *The Penguin Historical Atlas of the British Empire*, (2006)

For other locations:

PORTER, A.N. *Atlas of British Overseas Expansion*, Routledge 1991

Thank you to the Regimental Museum of the Royal Dragoon Guard at York for information on General Miles Staveley [hhg@rdgmuseum.org.uk]

Before the County reorganisation of the early 1970s, the River Ure was, in the Ripon area, the boundary between the North and West Ridings. The North Riding was for infantry, the traditional recruiting area for the Green Howards (19th of Foot) while the West Riding was the area for the West Yorkshire Regiment (14th of Foot). Several monuments in the Cathedral mention connections with the West Yorkshire Regiment.

Burke's Landed Gentry, Ridings of York.

World War I Memorials and the Reredos

Memorial Plaques to The Fallen in World War I

In addition to the inscribed names on the East Wall on either side of the High Altar to those men of Ripon who fell in the First World War, the north choir aisle in St Peter's Chapel contains the names of those who fell in the Second World War. There are further individual plaques to six of the former in the Cathedral nave but none for victims of the Second World War; why should this be so? It could be argued that there was a lack of wall space or that fashion had moved on since there are very few memorials of any kind dating beyond the 1920s. More profoundly, it is likely that the *modus operandi* of the Commonwealth War Graves Commission, with its establishment of standard headstones for all the fallen and there being no pecking order of rank, helped to promote a similar practice of commemoration in Churches and Cathedrals.

Nevertheless, it is satisfying to note that, of the six commemorated in Ripon Cathedral, there is one to a private soldier despite the other five being to officers. Of the six, only four are to men who might be truly regarded as Riponians, three of whom served in the same regiment. Two of the six were decorated for gallantry, one being awarded the exceptional combination of the VC, DSO and MC. These six are as follows:

Lt Col Neville Bowes Elliott-Cooper VC, DSO, MC (south nave aisle)

Neville Elliott-Cooper was the great-grandson of Captain J Elliott RN of Elliott House (now Holmefield House), Harrogate Road, Ripon and who had circumnavigated the globe under the command of Captain Cook. This would appear to be Neville's only connection with Ripon. His father, Robert Elliott-Cooper, was awarded the KCB in December 1918, having been Chairman of the War Office Committee on Hutted Camps during the war. Neville went from Eton to Sandhurst, from where he was commissioned as a Second Lieutenant in October 1908. He joined the Royal Fusiliers (City of London Regiment) and was a Lieutenant when war broke out. He was gazetted firstly as a temporary Captain from January 1915, then as a temporary Major in the September and finally (as a holder of the Military Cross) as a temporary Lt Colonel and Battalion Commander from July 1916! He was serving on the Western Front near Cambrai (formerly spelt Cambray) when he saw action leading to the award of the Victoria Cross. The following entry appeared in *The London Gazette* on 12th February 1918:

Courtesy of Royal Fusiliers Association

Lt. Col. Neville Bowes
Elliott-Cooper, VC, DSO, MC

"**For most conspicuous bravery and devotion to duty.**
Hearing that the enemy had broken through our outpost line, he rushed out of his dug-out, and on seeing them advancing across the open he mounted the parapet and dashed forward calling upon the Reserve Company and details of the Battalion Headquarters to follow. Absolutely unarmed, he made straight for the advancing enemy, and under his direction our men forced them back 600 yards. While still some forty yards in front he was severely wounded.
Realising that his men were greatly outnumbered and suffering heavy casualties, he signalled to them to withdraw, regardless of the fact that he himself must be taken prisoner.By his prompt and gallant leading he gained time for the reserves to move up and occupy the line of defence."
His DSO citation states: "For rallying his battalion when it had become temporarily disorgansed, and for leading forward a patrol of twenty men under very heavy fire and returning to his Brigadier with twenty prisoners and very valuable information", whilst that for his MC says: "For conspicuous ability in organising an attack on 15th April 1916, and consolidating craters subsequently gained. He has shown great ability in many difficult situations."

He died in captivity at the hospital of No 1 (Reserve) Prisoner of War Camp, Hanover on 11 February 1918, aged 29, (having received his wounds on 30 November 1917) and is buried in Hamburg Cemetery, Hanover.

Lt Hanley Hutchinson (north nave aisle)

Hanley Hutchinson was the son of William Hanley and Elizabeth Clare Hutchinson of The Meads, South Crescent, since demolished and replaced by the present Anchor retirement housing. He qualified as a solicitor in October 1913 and worked with his father until he joined the Army and was commissioned into the 5th Battalion, West Yorkshire Regiment (Prince of Wales's Own). Had he lived, he would have been an uncle to Michael Hutchinson of Hutchinson & Buchanan, Solicitors, in North Street. He received fatal wounds while serving in the Somme region of the Western Front and died on 1 September 1917 aged 26. He is buried at Grevillers (mis-spelt on his memorial), a large war cemetery, near to Bapaume.

Lt Ingleby Stuart Jefferson RN (north nave aisle)

Ingleby Jefferson's memorial attracts much attention because it includes an accurate facsimile of a naval officer's sword. He was the son of Dr William Dixon and Mary Stuart Jefferson of North House, Ripon – which remains a medical practice to this day. His family and the Hutchinsons were friends so he would have known Hanley Hutchinson well; they were to die less than six weeks apart.

As can be seen from the photograph on the cover, Ingleby Jefferson was a striking looking man. He played rugby for the Royal Navy. At the start of the war he was serving in a Torpedo Boat, but after having had his appendix removed, he volunteered, for submarines. In January 1915, he saved a soldier from drowning in Immingham docks and was awarded the Royal Humane Society's Bronze Medal (on the photo you can see this medal, which is worn on the right side, whereas military medals are worn on the left side).

Ingleby was only 24 when in command of HM Submarine C34. These were early days for submarine operations and many in the Navy did not consider their deployment to be proper! It is perhaps for this reason that early boats (as submarines are known) were given just numbers rather than names. There were 38 C class boats built but C34, built at Chatham Dockyard, was the last to enter service, in September 1910. Her complement was 2 officers and a ship's company of 17 in a vessel just over 142 ft long with a beam of 13ft 7in and a draft of 11ft 6in. This class was the last to be built with a petrol rather than a diesel engine. Her early career was inauspicious as in 1913 she was involved in a collision with the battle-cruiser HMS Invincible, later to be lost with all but six of her ship's company of 1021 at the Battle of Jutland.

C34 was torpedoed whilst on the surface 59 miles east of Fair Isle on 21 July 1917 by the German U52. There was only one survivor, a stoker, who was picked up by U52. Ingleby Jefferson's name is listed on the Naval War Memorial in Portsmouth.

Lt Ingleby Stuart Jefferson RN

Above: memorial with ceremonial sword

Right: Jefferson's submarine with crew

Courtesy of Mr Ingleby Jefferson

IN AFFECTIONATE MEMORY
OF
THOMAS·CROW·KIRK
AGED·17. A·PRIVATE·IN·THE
9TH·BATTN·WEST·YORKS·REGT
YOUNGEST·SON·OF
WILLIAM·WILKS AND ISABELLA·KIRK
OF·THIS·PARISH.
KILLED·IN·ACTION
AFTER LANDING AT SUVLA BAY
6TH AUGUST 1915,
DURING THE GREAT WAR
1914-1918.
"GREATER LOVE HATH NO MAN
THAN THIS."

Pte Thomas Crow Kirk (south nave aisle)

Thomas Kirk was born in 1898 at Quarry Moor but later lived with his family at 7 Littlethorpe Terrace – now part of Knaresborough Road. Although his memorial might give the impression that he was illegitimate, his parents were William Wilks Kirk and Isabella Kirk who had 7 children of whom Thomas was the youngest His father came from Westwick (between Bishop Monkton and Roecliffe) and his mother from Horsforth.

Like Hanley Hutchinson, Thomas also joined the West Yorkshire Regiment (Prince of Wales Own) – Ripon at that time being in the West Riding of Yorkshire - but in the 9th Battalion. Aged only 17, he was shipped out to the Dardanelles and was killed in action after the landings at Suvla Bay on 6 August 1915. He is commemorated on the War Memorial at Helles in Turkey.

Lt Col Ronald Harcourt Sanderson (north nave aisle)

Born 11 December 1876 at the Vicarage, High Hurstwood, Uckfield, Sussex, the son of Rev. Prebendary Edward and Mary Jane Sanderson, Ronald Sanderson was a regular soldier in the Royal Field Artillery. His connection with Ripon is that he was Commandant of the Royal Artillery Command Depot at Ripon from 1 July 1917 to 18 February 1918. Ripon, at that time, was a large holding and training depot for the Army and occupied much of the land to the west of the City. After serving in Ripon, he was sent to the Western Front and was killed, aged 41, whilst serving with the 148th Brigade, Royal Field Artillery, on 17 April 1918 at Scherpenberg Kemmel in Flanders aged 41. He is buried in Lijssenthoek Military Cemetery which is about 8 miles West of Ypres.

His memorial in the Cathedral also commemorates all other men of the Royal Artillery who fell in the Great War.

2nd Lt Reuben Addison Mangin MM (south nave aisle)

Reuben Mangin was born on 15 December 1885, the second son of Edward Addison and Katherine Mangin. Edward, who died in 1925 aged 70, was a retired major and has a separate memorial near to his son's. The family lived in Bishopton Grove,

Bishopton, Ripon until the 1930s. Reuben joined the army as a Private Soldier in the Infantry and was listed as such when awarded his Military Medal 'for bravery in the field' whilst serving with the Canadian Contingent. This appeared in the *London Gazette* of 27 October 1916, but there is no record of what would presumably have been the award of a field commission, between that date and his being wounded on 26 March 1918. At his death from his wounds on 7 April 1918 at the age of 32, he was listed as serving with the 2nd Battalion, West Yorkshire Regiment (Prince of Wales's Own). He is buried in St Sever Cemetery just outside Rouen. This is another large cemetery (over 3000 burials) on the South East side of the City adjacent to numerous military hospitals situated there for the entirety of the War.

Bishopton Grove (pictured in 2008); once the home of the Mangin family

John Wimpress

Notes and Sources

London Gazette 1909 – 1918

Commonwealth War Graves Commission

1901 Ripon Census

We thank Maj Gen Geoffrey Collin for his research

We thank Mr Michael Hutchinson for his information on Lt. Hanley Hutchinson and likewise Mr Ingleby Jefferson for information regarding Lt Ingleby Stuart Jefferson

The Reredos

The splendid reredos (decorated screen) behind the high altar under the east window was designed by Sir Ninian Comper as a memorial to the Fallen in WWI and installed in 1922. The names of 250 men and one woman are carved into the stone arcading on either side of the reredos. It took more than a year for all the statues to be added, as the reredos fund had become depleted and they had to wait for individuals to sponsor figures (the larger ones cost £76 each and the smaller ones £28). The reredos, which cost over £3,000, was championed by the Dean of the time, the Very Rev. Charles Mansfield Owen, who developed a good working relationship with Comper over the years.

The Dean wrote numerous letters and held many events to raise the necessary funds, not an easy task during the lean post-war years. In a speech made during such a fundraising event, reported in the Ripon Observer, the Dean outlined his reasons for supporting such an expensive undertaking: "...nothing could be too good to commemorate the splendid service and willing sacrifices of those who died that we might live – they had saved others, themselves they could not save. The reredos would commemorate no less than 260 gallant men of Ripon who laid down their lives to bring about the peace of the world..." The Dean added that they were custodians to a great inheritance, and he could not allow any permanent addition to be made to the structure of the Cathedral unless the work itself was the very best that could be put in, and the design made and carried out by one of the first architects of the day.

The sculptor commissioned by Comper was William D Gough, with whom he had worked before. The figures were carved from stone, with alabaster faces and hands, in his studio and then transferred to the Cathedral, where they were painted *in situ* by the ecclesiastical painter HAB Bernard–Smith.

Comper was an ecclesiastical architect and artist. His unique style was influenced by Anglo - Catholic Churchmanship, the Gothic Revival and to some extent the Arts and Crafts Movement. He believed that the artistic expression of the late Middle Ages, which centred so profoundly on the spiritual, was an ideal to be aspired to. Christian symbolism is a language accessible to all, including the illiterate. During the Middle Ages, art was never considered an end in itself, but always contained a mystical or spiritual meaning

For people to judge medieval art by the standards applied to the art of other periods is misleading. A naturalistic representation of the figure was not the highest aim. The medieval Church, the major patron of the arts at the time, considered the Church's purpose to be the redemption of God's creation. Art was promoted only to the extent that it would encourage man to seek Christ's salvation. The gaze of the saints, painted or sculpted, was firmly on the next world, the kingdom of God. That is why the best of medieval art has an ethereal, symbolic quality, which Comper sought to recreate in his work.

To one side of Christ, on the top tier of the reredos, is a carving of the Archangel Michael, the general of the heavenly host, fighting in the cosmic battle between good and evil. Perhaps surprising is his look of concentration and reflection, determination yet repose. He is not fired-up with a temporary adrenaline rush or brutish anger. To defeat the ultimate evil requires more than that and this carving of the archangel reflects the importance and intensity of this battle with delicate subtlety.

Flanking the figure of the risen Christ on the other side is St George, a warrior saint, representing the martial aspect of the reredos as a war memorial. Both Michael, the general of the heavenly host, and St George, soldier and patron saint of England, are slaying dragons, a medieval symbol of evil. St George is defeating physical evil, whilst St Michael is overcoming spiritual evil. Some believe the youthfulness of the risen Christ (no beard) to be a reflection of the young age at which many of the men commemorated here were, when they died.

10 larger and 9 smaller figures make up the lower tier. The theme in the selection of saints is the history of the Christian Church in the North of England representing both the Roman and the Celtic mission. In the centre is a statue of the Blessed Virgin Mary holding the infant Jesus. According to Comper, this is based on a medieval carving which is situated in the Chapter House at York Minster. On either side of the reredos on the east wall are the figures of St Peter and St Wilfrid, the patron saints of Ripon Cathedral.

Courtesy of Imperial War Museum

VAD Katharine Kinnear

The only woman commemorated in the WWI reredos inscriptions is **Katharine Ferrars Kinnear**, VAD (Voluntary Aid Detachment). In fact she was a nurse with the St John Ambulance Unit and it is the British Red Cross emblem combined with that of the Order of St John which is engraved on her headstone in Malo-Les Bains Communal Cemetery, France. This also bears the personal inscription "Until the day breaks". Katharine was born in Ripon, the daughter to the Rev. Henry G. Kinnear and Mrs Kinnear of Copgrove Rectory, near Knaresborough. She was awarded a Diploma by the French Government in recognition of her services. She died of enteric fever whilst nursing at Dunkirk on the 3rd September 1917, aged 29.

Toria Forsyth-Moser

Sources and Notes

The discrepancy between the 260 men mentioned by the Dean and the 250 actually commemorated can be explained by the reported refusal of the Catholic priest (during those not so ecumenical times) to allow his parishioners to be included in this memorial.

Project Correspondence in The Comper Papers at the RIBA Archive, V& A, London.

Sir Ninian Comper, Anthony Symondson and Stephen Bucknall, 2006.

We thank Jim Strawbridge for information regarding Katharine Kinnear.

The Display of Heraldry:

Arms on Ripon Cathedral Monuments

The application of coats of arms to monuments is a centuries-old practice, and is found in most churches and all cathedrals. The bearing of arms (heraldry) goes back to the twelfth century, when there was a need for personal recognition in wars, and has continued to the present day. It is used by families, corporate bodies like schools, local and ecclesiastical authorities, and is even attributed to real pre-heraldic or fictitious figures of the past, such as saints.

There is some control in England and Wales by the College of Arms, though there has always been 'false' heraldry which people have assumed without authority. Examples of all types of heraldry are found in Ripon Cathedral, providing a colourful addition to the Cathedral's interior. Heraldry has a language of its own, and some technicalities must be mastered; this is not too hard. Heraldry is not truly symbolic, with half-hidden meanings. There can be puns, even jokes, but on the whole heraldry is a stylised art. The technicalities of heraldry are covered later in this article, but first we will look at Ripon's own display of heraldry.

Heraldry in Ripon Cathedral

The heraldry in Ripon's Cathedral was created in various ways. The authorities would be responsible for some, like the east window in the 17th century, parts of which are now in the library, or the west window in the late 19th century, or the list of bishops in the nave. The local authority might put in some heraldry. In a town like Ripon, very conscious of its governance, it would be natural for a monument like that to the last Wakeman to be put up, at its expense. The arms at the top of this monument are puzzling, incidentally, apparently two bars dancetty and a chief per fess (1) - *the numbers refer to the images in this chapter.* Is it an example of punning

Arms of the first
Wakeman, Hugh Ripley

heraldry, with a 'ripple' effect, for Mr Ripley? We shall see other puns in heraldry later.

Very often it would be the families worshipping in the Cathedral who paid for whatever was shown, particularly in family monuments. The elaborate heraldic window to the Nortons in the north aisle, for example, (11) was commissioned by the third Lord Grantley from the foremost heraldic window artist of the day, Thomas Willement. Consultations would take place, and the families would give information to the artist to prepare the work to their satisfaction. It would be rarely that the artist would enquire further about what he was told. One may wonder quite how Commander Elliott knew that he was entitled to the traditional Elliott arms he displayed on his silverware, and appear later on his monument (25). His ancestry has never quite been explained.

There is nothing unusual about the display of the heraldry in Ripon Cathedral. Arms are attached to the monuments in the accepted manner – on brasses they are incised, or enamelled in more modern times (28). On stone or marble monuments great achievements may be splashed – the large monument in the south west tower is typical, where Sir Edward Blackett of Newby, the second baronet, lies back in glory, with his heraldry above (20).

In medieval times they had been more sober – as with the two Markenfield tombs in the north transept, where the arms of the Markenfields mix with those of their wives and other powerful noble families they wished to honour. There are quite a few modest heraldic monuments in Ripon, where the artist will quietly have delineated his version of the heraldry (2).

Windows

The best heraldry in Ripon Cathedral is to be found in its windows. The glorious colours of heraldry are able to gleam through the light of the glass. An early 14th century shield is to be found in the most westerly window of the south aisle (3). These are a version of the arms of England, and probably represent John Earl of Cornwall's arms.

There are various pieces in the north aisle, some rescued from obscurity. Three show the arms of Wentworth (4), Swales (5) and Hutton (6) and date from the seventeenth century. One item would seem to relate to the magnificent Dininckhoff glass of the Procters at Fountains Hall.

There is an excellent collection of heraldic glass in the east window of the library, up the stairs in the south transept. Part of this was in the chancel east window, and some was re-arranged here by Willement, the artist already mentioned. There is work here from the best heraldic artists of their time, Henry Gyles and William Peckitt, both of York. Dates here vary from 1713 to 1836.

A collection of arms of various local and even national people was created here. To note a few – the Aislabies of Studley Royal (7), Mrs Lawrence (52) who was their heiress, William Weddell of Newby Hall (8), whose non-heraldic monument is noticed elsewhere, William Markham, Archbishop of York 1777-1807, (9) and William van Mildert, Bishop of Durham 1826-36 (10). The arms of Bishop Porteus, noted in the article on Ripon and the Empire for his anti-slavery work, are also found, impaled by his see. A number of the arms give the names with the abbreviation Arm., which

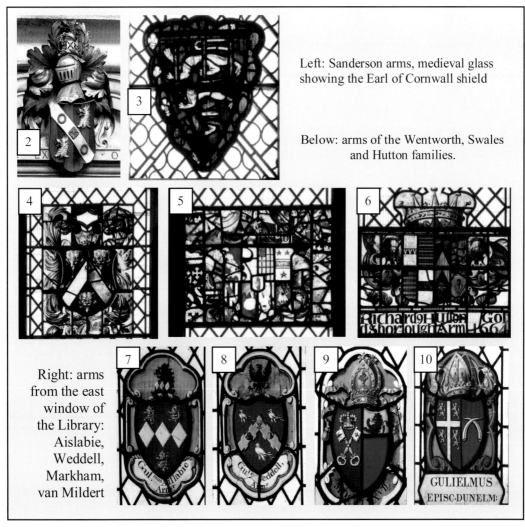

Left: Sanderson arms, medieval glass showing the Earl of Cornwall shield

Below: arms of the Wentworth, Swales and Hutton families.

Right: arms from the east window of the Library: Aislabie, Weddell, Markham, van Mildert

means armiger, arms bearer. The bearing of arms was clearly regarded as important. There are other fragments of early glass in south windows in the library including bits of royal arms which are probably another commemoration of James I's connection with Ripon.

The most magnificent window, however, is that to the Nortons, Barons Grantley, in the north aisle, of 1840, by Willement (11). As he liked, it is purely heraldic, without any religious content. The magnificent quartered shield is surrounded by historical references, to Edward III, the houses of Lancaster and Westmoreland, and the Nevilles, all adding to the pomp of the Nortons. At the top of the window are various heraldic badges.

Detail from the Norton (Grantley) window in the nave

Further aristocratic heraldry is found in the north choir aisle, where two windows celebrate scions of the Robinson/Vyner family, whose brother-in-law was the first Marquess of Ripon (1827-1909), of Studley Royal. On these windows, which are rather fading, may be seen the six quarters used by the marquess, with the young men's own simpler family coat (Vyner: Azure, a bend or; on a chief or, two Cornish choughs proper), bearing the differences (cadency marks) demanded by current practice – a crescent for the second son and a martlet (small bird) for the fourth (12, 13). One notes, in the Robinson coats, the change from an earl's coronet to that of a marquess, the change in his status occurring in 1871 (14, 15). The young men both died in 1870.

R. A Vyner (12),
F.G. Vyner (13)

Robinson, Earl of Ripon (14), Robinson, Marquess of Ripon (15)

Monuments

Heraldry on monuments can suffer from flaking paint and bad restoration, which on the whole has been avoided in Ripon. As mentioned above a coat of arms would be aded to the monument, from evidence supplied by the family, who might want its appearance to be identical or allow the designer artistic freedom. The display was to show the gentility of the family, that they were gentry or in some cases here, of course, even higher, as in the case of the Markenfield tombs (16). Heraldry is liberally scattered round the tombs of both the Markenfield knights, in the usual manner of medieval tombs. These arms would have been fully coloured in their time, as would have been the arms on the surcoat and sword of the stylish Sir Thomas Markenfield. Not all the heraldry has been identified, but that of the Neville, Soothill (17), Roos (18), Scrope, and Goldsborough families can certainly be seen. In some cases there are marriage connections, in others simply the desire to associate the Markenfields with other prominent gentry of the north. On the earlier, less bulky, tomb the knight has a unique collar of a hart in palings (19), the meaning of which has caused much discussion (see pages 28-9, 34).

Two seventeenth century monuments which might have contributed notable heraldry are those of Moses Fowler in the south choir aisle, which probably did once have arms, and that to Dean Anthony Higgin in the library. This does have heraldry, but its restoration has left us a travesty of the arms, some of which were not even in existence in Higgin's time.

A little later than these is the elaborate monument to Sir Edward Blackett, baronet, of Newby Hall, who died in 1718. His arms (20) are at the top, complete with baronet's badge, the red hand on a small shield (inescutcheon), also found on another Blackett monument (56). Other notable monuments include those of the 17th century to some of the Aislabie (21) and the Mallorie (22) family members, in

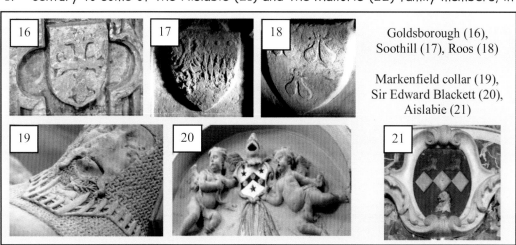

Goldsborough (16), Soothill (17), Roos (18)

Markenfield collar (19), Sir Edward Blackett (20), Aislabie (21)

the stairs outside the library. The comparative simplicity of the earlier heraldry contrasts with later elaborate work. The Floyer monument (nave, south side, near the altar), has what may be called a typical approach to heraldry. The monument (23, 24) is elegant and quite simple, and the arms are simply popped in at the bottom, without fuss.

The John Elliott (d.1834) Gothic Revival monument in the baptistery, south aisle (25), shows uncoloured arms at the top, with the simple coat of a baton on a bend, impaled with the quarterly arms of his wife Isabella Todd. Her basic coat is Argent, three fox's heads erased gules, which incorporates the pun of tod = fox. The fourth quarter, for Bowes has another punning reference. The hatching on the heraldry here shows that it was not painted in colour.

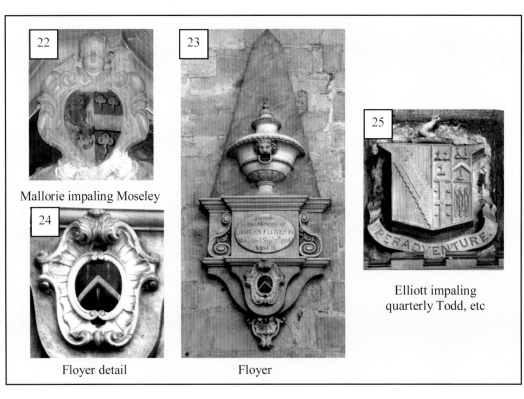

Mallorie impaling Moseley

Floyer detail

Floyer

Elliott impaling
quarterly Todd, etc

Other families who made puns are the Bowmans (26) and the Baynes (=bones) in the south aisle (27) and the brass to Canon Badcock (north transept) (28). Although there are many floor-slabs in the Cathedral, there is not one which displays heraldry, in contrast to some other Cathedrals. There are no early heraldic monumental brasses in the floor of Ripon Cathedral, though a few much later heraldic examples occur on the walls.

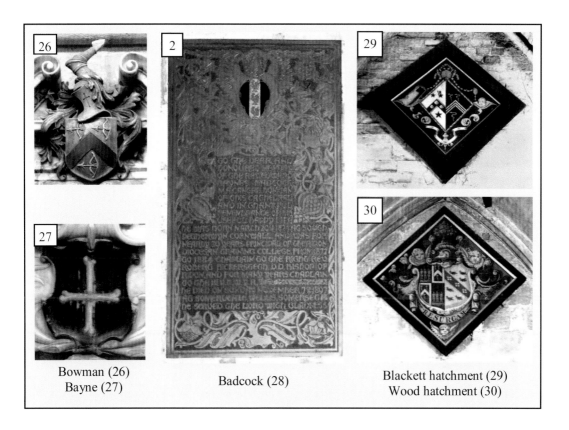

Bowman (26)
Bayne (27)

Badcock (28)

Blackett hatchment (29)
Wood hatchment (30)

Hatchments

These diamond-shaped panels were put up over the house of a man or woman entitled to bear arms, upon that person's death, and often were later displayed in the church. There are two of these in Ripon Cathedral; there were others, including one over the non-heraldic tomb of William Weddell. (Neo-classicism was not friendly to heraldry). The hatchment custom is rarely found today. There are various conventions whereby the sex and status of the deceased can be told, notably the background to the panels where black appears behind the arms of the deceased. In the case of Mrs Blackett (29), who died in 1788 (north transept), her background is black, but so is that of her husband, but we know it is she who has died, for there is no crest.

Henry Richard Wood, who died in 1844 (library staircase), has the black background, but his wife was still alive, and the background to her arms is white. He also has the full accoutrements in his hatchment, crest, motto etc. (30). The motto of RESURGAM (I shall rise again) is typical of usage on hatchments, and was not the family motto of the Woods. Both these hatchments are on the small side. Masham and Ripley churches have very good sets of larger hatchments.

Fabric

Arms were often incorporated in the fabric of the church, of patrons who may well have contributed to the cost of building, or who should be recognized. In Ripon the arms of Pigott occur more than once (31, 32), and two archbishops, Thomas Savage (1501-7) (south aisle) (33) and Cardinal Christopher Bainbridge (1508-14) (north aisle) (34) are commemorated. The latter includes the cardinal's hat above the shield. Bainbridge is probably the only murder victim commemorated in the Cathedral. In a moment of temper Bainbridge had struck his bursar, a priest, and the priest's revenge was to poison his master. The presence of such arms can be

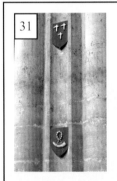 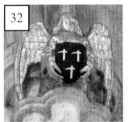  

Various arms appear on parts of the cathedral structure: e.g. on a pillar (left) or as corbels in the nave.
Pigott and Ripon (31), Pigott (32), Savage (33) and Bainbridge (34)

useful in dating building work.

The arms of Fountains Abbey (35) appear on a similar corbel to those of Savage and Bainbridge; the abbey would be close to its dissolution when these were put up. A series of arms appears on the pulpitum, which forms the entrance to the chancel. Among these is another Pigott (36) coat and that of the prominent Ward family (37), with the cross.

Both the transepts have monochrome arms at a high level, on corbels. These are of local families and are quite modern. There are blank shields in the chancel, south side, and on the font. I suspect the latter were just decorative, but one may wonder whether those in the chancel had the arms of contributors to the fabric – trade guilds for instance.

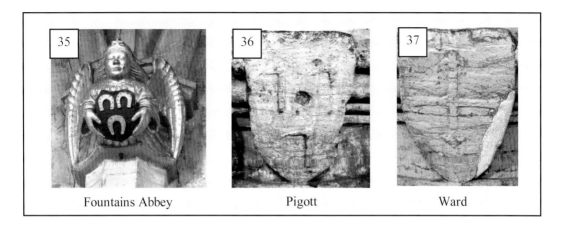

| 35 | 36 | 37 |
| Fountains Abbey | Pigott | Ward |

Royal Arms

The arms of the sovereign were frequently to be found in church buildings, but the practice of putting up royal arms in paintings or three-dimensional carvings became mandatory in the sixteenth century and has continued since. There is an excellent example in Ripon, that of James I (38), whose association with Ripon has long been celebrated. It is unusual in having the motto BEATI PACIFICI (Blessed are the peacemakers), which was often used by James instead of the more normal DIEU ET MON DROIT. This example is also rare in having an apparent practice painting on its reverse. There is of course a statue of James in the north transept/crossing, another in the choir screen, and portions of a Stuart royal arms appear in the library windows (south side).

Bishops and Deans

There are few arms of the twelve bishops or the fifteen deans of the modern Cathedral, or their families, though many of them did bear arms. On the whole the bishops have their monuments and heraldry elsewhere, having moved on. Examples which do occur are those of the first two bishops Bickersteth and Longley in the west window, and of Bishop Boyd Carpenter in a north aisle window by Sir Ninian Comper. The Bickersteth arms also appear in a window in the north choir aisle. Dean Erskine has a window in the south aisle, and there are modern heraldic monuments

103

to Deans Mansfield Owen and Birchenough in the Chapel of the Holy Spirit, east of the south choir aisle.

Corporate Heraldry

Corporate bodies as well as families may have heraldry granted, and there are a few in the Cathedral. Ecclesiastical bodies often do, and Ripon Diocese is no exception. The diocese was created in 1836, and very quickly a grant of arms was obtained from the College of Arms. A very nice simple coat was chosen: Argent, on a saltire gules, two keys in saltire or, wards upwards; on a chief gules, a paschal lamb proper, and is found throughout the Cathedral (39, 40).

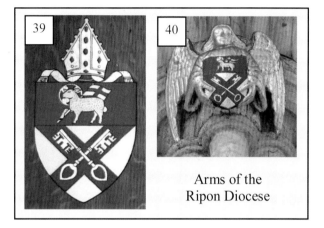

Arms of the
Ripon Diocese

The arms of York Diocese also are found here, but not as commonly as one might have expected. Bishops were allowed to impale the arms of their diocese before their own (41, 42). The city's arms appear here and there in the Cathedral (43, 44). These arms have never been officially granted, but have been commonly used for centuries. They may be described as Gules, a stringed horn or, the bow surrounding the letters R.I.P.P.O.N. The monument to Dean Birchenough shows the arms of Oriel College, Oxford (45), rather than family arms.

Attributed Heraldry

There is not a great deal of heraldry attributed to pre-heraldic or fictitious people in Ripon, but one prominent example is on the elaborate 1913 pulpit by Henry Wilson. This includes the arms of St Cuthbert (lions) (46), St Hilda (snakes) (47), Etheldreda (crowns) (48) and Chad (crosses paty) (49). One might have expected the 'arms' of St Wilfrid to have been here, Azure, three estoiles or, but they are found elsewhere in the Cathedral (50). St William of York's arms Or, seven mascles gules, also appear in the fabric, both in the north and south aisles, on corbels (51), reflecting the close association of Ripon Minster with York Cathedral.

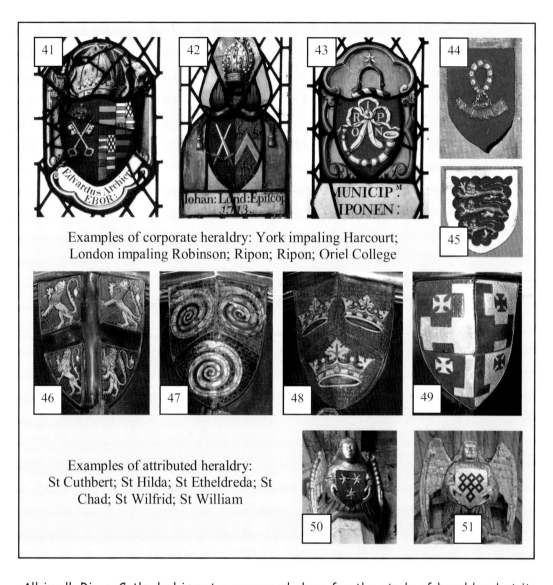

Examples of corporate heraldry: York impaling Harcourt;
London impaling Robinson; Ripon; Ripon; Oriel College

Examples of attributed heraldry:
St Cuthbert; St Hilda; St Etheldreda; St
Chad; St Wilfrid; St William

All in all, Ripon Cathedral is not a renowned place for the study of heraldry, but it does have examples of most heraldic practices, and there are some excellent pieces. This article does not mention all the armorial bearings which occur in the Cathedral – for instance the silver on display in the Treasury (north choir aisle) often has the arms of former owners, and the Cathedral regalia often bears arms. Ripon is short, in comparison with some other Cathedrals, of large elaborate monuments plastered with heraldry. It has also, like most Cathedrals, suffered from losses. The literature names quite a lot of heraldic monuments which have disappeared, but its windows are excellent, even if here too, there have been losses.

Heraldry

Technicalities of Heraldry

This is a brief note on terms such as shield (which is not always shield-shaped), crest (which is the object which appears above the arms, usually on a wreath, that is twisted colours, on a helmet), motto, mantling (the torn flowery or cloth material which is at the sides of the shield) and, for peers, the supporters, which are the animals holding the shield.

Heraldry uses the French language in part, though the terms tend to be pronounced in an English manner. The field (background) of the arms must be described first; there are metals - or (gold) and argent (silver), tinctures (colours) - gules (red), azure (blue), sable (black), vert (green), purpure (purple), and furs (ermine and vair). Charges in their true colours are described as 'proper'. Fields may be divided vertically, horizontally, quarterly, diagonally, or by chevron. The division lines may be straight or engrailed, nebuly, indented. A very simple blazon of a coat would be 'Azure, a chevron or', or 'Argent, a cross gules'. A basic, almost unbreakable, rule is that colour must be placed on metal and never on another colour, and metals similarly must not be placed on metals. This rule applies throughout the whole coat of arms, and is to make the coat easier to read.

The main charges (called ordinaries) are the pale, the fess, the bend, the bend sinister, the cross, the saltire, the chief and the pile. The first three have diminutives – pallets, bars, bendlets, and if of an even number the field is described as paly, barry or bendy.

Besides the ordinaries there are many smaller charges which may appear on their own or be associated round the main feature. These are taken from the animal, vegetable and mineral kingdoms, as well as the purely decorative. Common charges include crosses, roundels (solid circles with different names for each colour), lozenges (diamond shapes), annulets (rings), mullets and estoiles (stars), cinquefoils, billets (small rectangles), natural objects such as fleurs-de-is and roses, birds, fish and other animals (buck, lion/leopard, bulls are perhaps the most common) either as full animals with various positions (rampant, passant etc) or as heads or limbs, fabulous animals (unicorns, griffins, wyverns), weapons like arrows and spears, and other objects (like horns). In fact, anything *can* appear in a coat of arms, though older heraldry will tend to be more stylised than modern, e.g. 'Argent, a bend between two lions' heads erased gules'. Erased means torn off rather than cut off in a straight line.

The coat of arms is the most important part of the design, and is unique to the members of a family, or the organisation, and legal cases have been brought against those who usurp another's arms. Arms are fairly easy to identify and guesswork should be avoided. Mottoes may be in any language and are free to be used by anyone. Puns are quite common in the choice of mottoes. Again, there are books which help to identify the users of a motto.

Helmets usually show the degree of a person from royalty through peers to baronets, down to simple gentlemen and women. Some are found in Ripon. Women have almost always been entitled to use family arms, which are usually immediately recognisable by being displayed on a lozenge (a diamond shape) – again this practice can be seen in the Cathedral (52).

Lawrence quartering Aislabie, on lozenge

Whitaker arms, hatched

Crests – and it is best to use this term in the narrow sense of the item above the helmet, rather than apply it to the whole 'achievement', which is the term for the "full monty" – are not unique to a family, though many are. Identification of a crest alone, without arms or motto, is not easy.

Most heraldry is colourful and here in Ripon Cathedral it is, but where colour cannot easily be expressed, a code is used – Argent is blank; Or has small dots; Gules vertical lines; Azure horizontal lines; Sable lines running both horizontally and vertically; Vert lines slanting from top left to bottom right; Purpure slanting the opposite. This is a sort of shading, known as hatching (25, 53), and is often used on brasses and silverware, both of which are found in Ripon. Hatching, is also common in printed materials where the actual colour cannot be shown.

How Heraldry is Shown

Heraldry may show (a) a basic coat, male (54, 55, 57) or female (52); (b) a simple marriage (58); (c) a marriage with a heraldic heiress (56); (d) further marriages; (e) quartered coats (30, 15). Taking these in turn the basic coat will usually be the family arms, perhaps with a 'difference'. Heraldically this means an indication that the person is not the head of the family. The most common difference is a 'label', usually a three pointed bar at the top of the arms but there is a whole hierarchy of differences. Women, as mentioned above, have their arms on a lozenge, and are likely to be spinsters if there is just the one coat. Women, as the unwarlike sex, are not wearing helmets, and do not usually display helmets and crests above their arms.

In the case of a simple marriage, the man's coat of arms impales that of his wife, i.e. the two go side by side, his on the left as you see it (though dexter in heraldic terms, bearing in mind that this would be right to the wearer), and hers on the right (sinister heraldically). If the wife has no brothers, she is a heraldic heiress, and her arms are placed on a small shield (inescutcheon) in the centre of her husband's, 'in pretence' as it is called. If there has been more than one marriage, a husband may choose to show his former (usually deceased) wife's arms as well as his later spouse's. He may show the two marriages to the sinister of his own, or may place their arms on either side of his own.

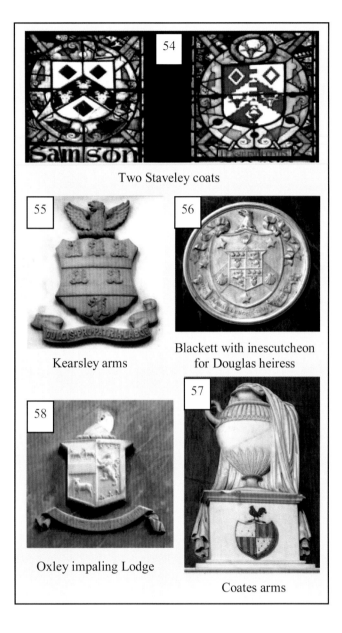

Two Staveley coats

Kearsley arms

Blackett with inescutcheon for Douglas heiress

Oxley impaling Lodge

Coates arms

Finally there are quartered arms, which figure prominently in heraldry. The best example in Ripon is in the north aisle window to the Norton Grantley family, where there are fifteen quarterings (11). These arise from marriages to heiresses, where the descendants of a man and his heraldic heiress wife show they represent her family by quartering her arms with their own. The first and fourth quarters have their family arms; the second and third the arms of their mother. If the mother's arms are already quartered (representing earlier heiress marriages) these arms will also be shown. Hence the numerous quarterings in the Norton shield.

David Lee

Notes and Sources

Books on heraldry are shelved in most libraries at Dewey class number 929.6.

BALMFORTH, Diana: *Ripon Cathedral stained glass* (1991)

DODSWORTH, Roger: *Yorkshire church notes*, edited by J.W.Clay (1904)

BLOOM, J.Harvey: *Heraldry in the churches of the West Riding of Yorkshire*, volume 6 (1895)

[FARRER, William]: *The history of Ripon...* (1801, 1806)

WALBRAN, J.R.: *A guide to Ripon...* (many editions, 19th century)

A pre-1660 etching of Ripon Cathedral with spires intact

The Graveyard

Above, Below and Within the Ground

For many visitors, the first sight of memorial stones at the Cathedral is the lawned graveyard with its ranks of stones and carvings. This is not so for those who approach through the great west doors, nor indeed for those scurrying in through the door in the north transept – for there are no gravestones to the west, nor the north of the Church.

A simple, but erroneous, explanation for this would be the layout of the current road system around the precinct; the real reason is however the cause of the road layout – not the result. Church graveyard burials were started in England around the 12th century and graves were created firstly on the south aspect, followed – when land ran out – by interments to the east of the building. Ripon was no different, placing its graveyard entirely to the south and east of the great Church and avoiding the northern and western land from where it was popularly believed that the devil emerged from the shadows.

Occupying around 4 acres, the graveyard has been extended by dedication of additional land, the last expansion being in 1858. Although now closed to new burials, – interments may still take place in family graves where space permits, although this is a rare occurrence at the Cathedral. The prevailing soil is sand with large amounts of gravel, making it a dry, freely draining site for graves. As with many old Churchyards, Ripon's graveyard has been subject to layer after layer of burials on top of previous occupants, with the date of first interments being lost in antiquity.

During the Middle Ages, there were a number of houses and yards to the immediate west of the present Cathedral entrance. Immediately inside the graveyard were reported to be a mortuary chapel, a well and a cross, this latter being the site for the reading of a Palm Sunday service. No sign of the chapel or well remain, but a stone stump at the south-west corner of the graveyard is reputed by some to be the remains of the cross.

General view of the graveyard
from the south east

Stump of a possible
medieval cross

Burials and Early Records

Since 1538 clergy of the Church of England and in Wales have kept, with varying degrees of thoroughness, registers of Church baptisms, marriages and burials. Thomas Cromwell, the Lord Chancellor to King Henry VIII, ordered the clergy of every parish Church in the land to keep a register book of all baptisms, marriages and burials. The register was required to be filled in every Sunday, in the presence of one of the Churchwardens, and was to be kept in a strong chest with two locks, the parson having one key and the other kept by the Churchwardens. Since many of these records were on loose leaf paper there are very few surviving records of early memorials. Here at Ripon, the effects of the Reformation were of much greater concern than mere record keeping – for example, Fountains Abbey was to surrender to the Crown in 1539 after many months of plotting and counter-plotting by the then Abbot of Fountains and Canon of Ripon, Marmaduke Bradley.

A lack of compliance with the 1538 Act was addressed by Queen Elizabeth through the Convocation of Canterbury of 1597. This ordered the parishes to purchase parchment registers, many of the old registers having decayed, and that the names from the original be copied into the new registers from the beginning, *"but especially since the first year of Her Majesty's reign."* This latter condition explains why many parish registers start from 1558, rather than 1538.

The bound, parchment registers still had to be completed every Sunday, but after 1597 this needed the presence of both Churchwardens as well as the parson and a third lock was added to the chest with each of the wardens having his own key!

Not content with having added a further layer of control to burial records, the 1597 Act also required the clergy to provide an annual summary to their Bishop (the so-called Bishop's transcripts). As with the first attempts at recording deaths in 1538, these transcripts were often only completed in part. Ripon's parish registers date from 1574 and are believed to be complete.

Examination of around 7,000 of the entries of burials in the Cathedral registers has helped identify events prior to 1634. The very first recorded interment (from the Registers) is for *"John Abbote, son of Edward of Ouldfield on 28 March 1574"* (Ouldfield now being known as Aldfield). In that first year a total of 66 burials were recorded, with numbers varying over ensuing decades. A sample of interments at 10 yearly intervals shows:

1574	1584	1594	1604	1614	1624
66	34	29	184	150	136

The Plague of 1625: a Legacy of John Lapthorne

Burial records show that in the immediate period following an outbreak of plague in 1625, at least 96 Ripon residents were buried in the Cathedral. Twenty-six of these were residents of Allhallowgate, and a further 20 were from the area of the Market Place. Also commemorated is the source of the plague: one John Lapthorne "a carryer to London" who had died in his lodging house, that of William Kyrkbies. It is further recorded that "He brought plague to the Town".

Apart from noting when the deceased was a widow, a pauper or a 'gent', the inscriptions are sparse. From 1604 further information is presented for some individuals. In that year for example, on 17 April Ann Houghton (alias Smithe) was buried, having been executed; 24 *"prysoners from Yorke"* were buried on 8 August and in October there were *"A number of plague deaths"*.

Other early commemorations include those who were buried after being executed:

Year	Date	Person	Cause of Death
1604	17th April	Ann Houghton (alias Smithe)	Executed
1605	5th September	William Brown of Hornby	Executed for treason
1608	5th October	George Kirbie	Prisoner, executed
1609	28th April	Matilda Allanson	Prisoner, executed
1609	4th October	Ralph Conyers & Elizabeth Carlton	Prisoners, executed
1626	17th April	Richard Abbay of Sawley	Hanged

Compassionate memorials are also recorded, with interments of the poor and unknown in the graveyard:

Year	Date	Person	Cause of Death
1606	24th August	A young man, a cripple	Dying at Sharow
1610	11th February	A child	Found by the waterside, drowned
1616	22nd December	A poor man from Bishopton	
1618	16th May	An old wife from Copt Hewick	
1622	28th September	A man	Found drowned at Nunwick
1623	14th December	A poor man and his begging wife died at Jo Dawson's in Allhallowgate	

Accidental deaths, whether by drownings or other accidents were also recorded:

Year Date	Person	Cause of Death
1608 — 29th April	Thomas & Mary Walker of Eveston	Drowned
1617 — 15th January	Richard Raynforth of Brecken Hall	Slain by a loaded wagon wheel going over him
1619 — 22nd January	Ralph Aker's maid of Sharow	Drowned in his well
1626 — 22nd August	Robert Ingram of Sharow	Killed with a horse
1627 — 31st August	Christopher Gyll of Market Place	Slain with a fall out of Mr Rypley's house top
1630 — 27th October	Ralph Bawland of Haddockstones	Slain by a sled drawn over him

In 1625 the effects of the plague were dramatic, with burials rising to 328 in that year.

The years 1630 to 1632 provide an interesting mystery from the Cathedral burial records in that three, unrelated, 'singing-men' were interred in that period. On 28th September 1630, Stephen Warlasse of Ripon was buried, having been killed by 'earth falling on him'; the following year on 11th January Richard Longassco 'a singing man of Ripon' was buried and in 1632, 7th July Emmaybie Mitchell 'a singing man' was also buried. What brought about this loss of musical talent in Ripon remains a mystery!

The political changes which accompanied the overthrow of the crown and the execution of Charles I in 1649, resulted in registration being temporarily taken out of the hands of the clergy and, in 1653, each parish appointed a lay "register" to keep the records. The earliest headstone located in the graveyard at Ripon commemorates several members of the wealthy Allanson family of Sharow and dates from c. 1625. (see Wilson, 1847).

(Following the restoration of Charles II in 1660, registration was again handled by the Church. Some clergy appear to have managed to re-construct the registers for the intervening period from a mixture of the "civil" registers, personal notes and their parishioners' memories. Without doubt, such registers are prone to error!)

Burial Practices

Interments at Ripon between 1666 and 1814 were subject to the Burial in Woollen Acts (1666 – two Acts, 1678 & 1680) which required the dead, except plague victims, to be buried in pure English woollen shrouds. These Acts were intended as unashamed trade protection measures in order to ensure "*the lessening the importation of linen from beyond the seas, and the encouragement of the woollen and paper manufactures of this Kingdom* ". Whilst there was widespread ignoring of the Acts from around 1770 onwards, it is reasonable to assume that the majority of graves in the Cathedral Churchyard dating from 1666 to the early 1800's contain woollen shrouded remains with or without a coffin. (An affidavit, which could be sworn before any person in Holy Orders, had to be brought within 8 days of the burial, under a penalty of £5, that the deceased was not buried in linen. Parish registers were marked with a note against the burial entries to confirm that affidavit had been sworn, or marked "naked" for those too poor to afford the woollen shroud.)

Poverty would also mean that some families did not bury their relatives in coffins, simply 'borrowing' the parish coffin for the burial service and then laying the remains to rest in just their shroud. A typical grave as reported from Ripon Cathedral in a survey to the Burial Acts Department in 1881 gives the area allocated to each grave as 7ft 3in x 3ft 3in, with a space of around 6in between graves. Accommodating from one to four bodies, they were excavated to a depth of between 6-12ft.

At that time, and serving a parish of around 5,000, it was expected that around 115 burials *per annum* would take place in the Churchyard. The southern approach to this 19th century graveyard was planted with an avenue of lime trees, from the south steps to the south transept door; the western limit had been progressively cleared of houses and dilapidated workshops between 1830 – 1882; and the purchase of additional land to the south and east in 1858 defined the graveyard as it is seen today.

Changes in the Style of Memorials

The earliest memorials (late 17th century.) at Ripon are simple upright slabs with inscriptions on (usually) the eastward facing aspect. Since the size, history and location of Ripon's Minster was of considerable repute, many of the merchants, dignitaries and landowners have been commemorated with large and expensive memorials.

The use in the 18th century of table tombs – hollow in the portion above ground – overcame problems of subsidence noted with the horizontal, flat slabs (ledger stones), many of which at Ripon have sunk into total obscurity. Tombs with the sides made of raised solid panels are usually referred to as altar tombs and Ripon has examples of both altar and table memorials.

More decorative pedestal-type memorials from the 19th century feature angels, crosses and urns and more recently the only memorial stones permitted have been those set in the ground so that grass maintenance is made more easy.

A table tomb (top)
and an altar tomb

The Bone House

Wilson, T. - see page 128

The undercroft before 1843; for some time, it was used as a bone repository. About 10,000 of these bones are now buried in the graveyard. The undercroft is now the Chapel of Resurrection.

It is necessary to explain one unusual memorial which is a pair of stones placed within the eastern wall of the graveyard. This commemorates many hundreds of previous interments which had, as was custom, been exhumed and the bones cleaned and stored in the undercroft at the Cathedral. Around 1843 the sexton at the Cathedral undertook a thorough sorting (and display) of the bones stored within the undercroft. The source of these somewhat grisly remains is thought to have been the many graves which were re-excavated during the early 16th century when the nave aisles were added to the Church.

This same sexton, Mr Thomas Wilson, is the individual who compiled and transcribed so many of the memorial inscriptions in 1847 and published his record as a valuable source document. By 1865, the decision was taken by Dean William Goode to inter many of these bones elsewhere in the graveyard. Accordingly a single pit was created at the eastern wall of the graveyard and some (though apparently not all) of the bones were buried together.

In this account from the 19th century, Francis Buckland

described his visit to the 'bone house' at Ripon

"Leaving the Chapter House, the verger conducted us to the crypt which is beneath it (now the Chapel of the Resurrection) Unlocking the massive door, we at once beheld a 'Golgotha' Bones were everywhere; skulls, arm bones, leg bones, skulls of old men, young men, women and children. The walls of the crypt are hidden behind a stack of bone six feet high and four feet thick. In former times they were scattered all about the vault but in 1843 the old sexton undertook the task of arranging them. He placed a row of skulls on the floor, then a row of arm and leg bones with the round ends protruding, then another of skulls and so on, till the space from floor to roof was fully occupied – the pillars of the crypt were ornamented with festoons of skulls – wherever there was a vacant space, a skull had been placed'.

The inscription on the memorial stones – now severely weathered - reads:

"Under this stone, in a pit 12 feet deep, the extent of which is marked out by boundary stones, a portion of the bones that were in a crypt under the south eastern part of the Cathedral were buried in May 1865."

Numbering around 10,000 the accumulated bones represent around 100 –120 years of burials at Ripon, making the burial pit in the Church yard among its oldest sites.

There are several legends surrounding this old relic house, not least of which is the story of a Ripon barber who used a partial skull as a shaving/lather dish. In mid-nineteenth century, this story was embroidered even further in the words of one William Harrison Ainsworth:

The Barber of Ripon and the Ghostly Basin:

a Tale of the Charnel House

by *William Harrison Ainsworth*

Since ghost-stories you want, there is one I can tell
Of a wonderful thing that Bat Pigeon befel;
A barber, at Ripon, in Yorkshire was he,
And as keen in his craft as his best blade could be.

Now Bat had a fancy - a strange one, you'll own, -
Instead of a brass bowl to have one of bone.
To the Charnel-house 'neath the Old Minster he'd been
And there, 'mongst the relics, a treasure had seen.

'Mid the pile of dry bones that encumber'd the ground,
One pumpkin-like skull with a mazard he'd found;
If home that enormous old sconce he could take,
What a capital basin for shaving 'twould make!

Well he got it, at last, from the Sexton, his friend,
Little dreaming how queerly the business would end;
Next, he saw'd off the cranium close to the eyes;
And behold then! a basin capacious in size.

As the big bowl is balance 'twixt finger and thumb,
Bat's customers all with amazement are dumb;
At the strange yellow object they blink and they stare,
But what it can be not a soul is aware!

Bat Pigeon, as usual, to rest went that night;
But he soon started up in a terrible fright;
Lo! giving the curtains and bedclothes a pull,
A ghost he beheld - wanting half of its skull!

"Unmannerly barber!" the Spectre exclaimed;
"To desecrate bonehouses art not ashamed?
Thy crown into shivers, base varlet, I'll crack,
Unless, on the instant, my own I get back!"

"There it lies on the table!" Bat quakingly said;
"Sure a skull cannot matter when once one is dead." -
"Such a skull as thine may not, thou addlepate fool!
But a shaver of crowns for a Knight is no rule!"

With this, the worth Spectre its brainpan clapp'd on,
And holding it fast, in a twinkling was gone;
But ere through the keyhole the Phantom could rush,
Bat perceived it had taken the soap and the brush.

When the Sexton next morn went the Charnel-house round,
The great Yellow Skull in its own place he found;
And 'twixt its lank jaws, while they grinningly ope,
As in mockery stuck, are the Brush and the Soap!

Andrew Coulson

Notes and Sources

"Transcript of Ripon Cathedral Burials 1574 – 1634, County Hall Northallerton"

Index

Numbers in **bold** show pages on which there are illustrations

Abbay, Richard, hanged 113

Abbote, John 112

Adam, Robert, architect 8, 66

Adams, John 69

Ainsworth, William Harrison, poem
118-19

Aislabie family 8, 54, 55; arms 97,
97, 99, **99**

Aislabie, John 15, 52-4, 84

Aker, Ralph 114

Allanson family 13, 114

Allanson, Matilda, executed 113

America 68-71

America, HMS 80

Anderson, John 17

Arbuthnot family 60, 61

arms *see* heraldry

Arts and Crafts style 9

attributed heraldry 104-5, **105**

Badcock, Canon Edward Baynes, arms
100, **101**

Bainbridge, Cardinal Christopher,
arms 102, **102**

Barberini Venus 67

Bawland, Ralph 114

Bayne, Hellen 20-1, **20**; arms **18**, 19,

100, **101**

Bell, Thomas 16

Bickersteth, Bishop Robert 41;
arms **18**, 19, 100, **101**

Birchenough, Dean Godwin 41, **43**;
arms 103, 104, **105**

bishops, 83-4; arms 103
see also under the names of
individual bishops, and under
clerical memorials

Blackett, Sir Edward, baronet 7, **7**,
46, 55-7, **56**, **65**, 66; arms 96,
99, **99**

Blackett, Elizabeth, hatchment 101,
101

bone house 116-19

Booth, Diana 55

Bowes arms 100, **100**

Bowland *see* Bawland

Bowman family, arms 100, **101**

Bowman, Thomas More 18-19, **18**

Bradley, Marmaduke, Abbot of
Fountains 111

Brafferton Hall, Virginia **73**

Brafferton Manor, Yorkshire 72-3

Braithwaite family 21, 58

brasses:

Canon Badcock 100, **101**

Jordan Crosland **46**

Robert Dawson 48-9, **49**

at Topcliffe 36

British Empire 75-85

Brown, William, executed 113

Browne, Lt Constantine 81-2, **81**

Bruce family 76

Buckland, Francis 117

burial in woollen 115

burial practices 115

calendar, Julian 20, 25-6

Carlton, Elizabeth, executed 113

Carpenter, Bishop William Boyd 11;
    arms 103

Carr, John, architect 66

Carrington, David 31

Cato the elder, quoted 6

Chad, St, attributed arms 104, **104**

chantries 28, 34, 36

Chapman, John 17

charnel house 116-19

charters, Ripon 48, 50

Chettle, Margaret 21-2

children on memorials 25-6

Christ see Jesus Christ

churchyard see graveyard

Civil War, English 6, 10, 30, 39, 44-7

Clark, Elizabeth 20

clerical memorials 38-43

Clough, Sarah and Harriet 21

Coates family 26; arms **108**

coats of arms see heraldry

Cock, Fanny 16

coffins 115

Collinson, Robert, signalman 23

Comper, Sir Ninian 9, **9**, 11, 91, 92,
93, 103

Convocation of Canterbury 111

Conyers family, arms 31

Conyers, Ralph, executed 113

Cook, Captain James 82

Cornforth, John 28

Cornwall, John, Earl of, arms 96, **97**

corporate heraldry 104, **104**

Crabtree family 12

Cromwell, Thomas 111

Crosland family 45, 46, 55

Crosland, Jordan 44-7, **46**, 66, 73

cross, medieval, possible, in Ripon
111, **111**

Crosse, Brian 34

Cuthbert, St, attributed arms 104,
105

dating: calendar problems 20, 25-6

Davis, Charles 17

Dawson, Jo 113

Dawson, Robert 47-50, **47**, **49**

deans, arms 103-4

Dene, Canon John 38

Dilessi (Greece), murders in 63-5

Dininckhoff, Baernard, glazier 96

Dowson, John 16

Durbin, Leslie 10

Edward IV, arms 98

Elizabeth I 111

Elliott, Commander John 8, 82-3, **82**, 86-7, **87**; arms 96, 100, **100**

Elliott, Sir William Henry 83

Elliott House (Holmefield House) **82**

Elliott-Cooper, Lt Col Neville Bowes 83, 86-7, **87**

Emmerson, Bill 24, 26

Emmerson, Jean 12, **12**, 24-5, **24**, **25**, 26

Empire *see* British Empire

epitaphs 13-18, *and see many in the chapter on women and children*

other significant epitaphs:

John Aislabie 54

Sir Edward Blackett 56

Jordan Crosland 46

Robert Dawson 49

Dean Moses Fowler 38

Elizabeth Garnett **23**

Edmund Jenings 70

Crow Kirk **90**

Sir Thomas Markenfield 31

Charles Oxley 57

Christopher Oxley 58

Emily Oxley 60

Robert Porteous 74

Hugh Ripley 50-1

William Slayter Smith 79

Francis William Waddilove 78

Robert James Darley Waddilove 80

Jemima Webber 40

William Weddell 65

Erskine, Dean Henry David, arms 103

Etheldreda, St, attributed arms 104, **105**

explorers 82-3

Featherstone, Jane 21

Fiennes, Lady Celia 55

Floyer, arms 100, **100**

Fountains Abbey, arms 102, **103** *see also* Bradley, Marmaduke

Fountains Hall 96

Fowler, Dean Moses 7, **7**, 38, 48, 99

Fox, George 45

Franklin, Benjamin 69

Fremantle, Dean William 41

funeral hatchments *see* hatchments

Galatea, HMS 76

Garnett, Elizabeth 19, **19**, 23-4, **23**; picture **24**

Gayer-Anderson, Theo 31

George, St 93-4, **93**

Gill *see* Gyll

glass, 10, **10**; *see also under* windows

Goddard & Gibbs 12, **12**

Goldsborough arms 99, **99**

Goode, Dean William 117

Gosney, Harold 10, **10**, **76**, 77

Gothic Revival style 8, 9, **9**

Gough, William D. 9, **9**, 92, **92**

Grand Tour 60, 66

Grantley, Lords *see* Norton

graveyard 110-19

Grayson, Joseph 14

Greece, terrorist murder 63-5

Green Howards 85

Gyles, Henry, glazier 97

Gyll, Christopher 114

Hall, The, Ripon *see* Minster House

Harcourt, Archbishop Edward
      Venables Vernon, arms **105**

Harper, Thomas 14

Harvey, Harry 11-12, **11**

hatching, heraldic 107, **107**

hatchments, funeral 101-2, **101**

Haynes, Charles 15

Helmsley Castle 44, **45**

Hemming, A.O., glazier 10

heraldry 95-109
      in Ripon Cathedral 95-105
      technicalities 106-9

Higgin, Dean Anthony 8, 39, **39**;

arms 99

Hilda, St, attributed arms 105, **105**

Hinde, William 73

Holmefield House (Elliott House) **82**

Hornblower, Ripon *see* Ripley, Hugh

Houghton, Ann, *alias* Smithe,
      executed 113

Hughes, Dean Frederick Llewelyn 42,
      76

Hutchinson, Lt Hanley 88

Hutton, arms 96, **97**

Iles, Francis 15

Ingram, Robert 114

Irish prince, and lion tomb 35

James I, arms 98, 103, **103**

Jefferson, Lt Ingleby Stuart 88-9,
      89

Jenings, Charles 69-70

Jenings, Edmund 68-71, **68**, 72

Jenings, Elizabeth 69-70

Jerome, St 37

Jesus Christ, on reredos 94; in
      window 12, **12**; statue **76**, 77

Julian calendar 20, 25-6

Kearsley family 59, 60; arms **108**

Kinnear, VAD Katharine Ferrars 94,
      94

Kirbie, George, executed 113

Kirk, Private Thomas Crow 90, **90**

Kyrkbies, William 112

Lapthorne, John 112

Lawrence, Mrs Elizabeth, arms 97,
     107

Lawson, John 12, **12**

Le Grice, Dean Edwin 11, **11**

ledger stones 116

Lee, Robert E, 70

library, cathedral 39

lion tomb 34-7, **35**

London Diocese, arms **105**

Longassco, Richard 114

Longley, Caroline 24

Longley, Bishop Charles 24, 41, **41**;
     arms **41**, 103

Lupton family 13

Lyndall, Christopher 48

Mallorie family 8; arms 99, **100**

Mangin, 2nd Lt Reuben Addison 90-1

March, Mary and Hannah 14

Markenfield family 7, 27-33, **28**, **29**;
     heraldry 30, 31, 96, 99, **99**

Markenfield collar 28-9, **29**, 34, 99,
     99

Markenfield Hall 27, **27**

Markham, Archbishop William, arms
     97, **97**

Marmion, Sir John 28

Mary, Virgin, statue **76**, 77

Masham church 102

medieval tombs 27-37

memorials:
     general reviews 5-6, 7-12
     in graveyard 115-16
     heraldry on 99-100

metal memorials 10

Metcalfe, Deborah 20

Metham arms 30

Michael, Archangel 93-4, **93**

Middleton arms 29

Milburn, William 13-14

Mildert, Bishop William van, arms
     97, **97**

military memorials 86-91; reredos
     91-4

Miniott arms 30

Minster House, Ripon 58

Mitchell, Emmaybie 114

monuments see memorials

Moorman, Bishop John 42, **42**

Muncaster, Lord 63

'Navvies Friend' see Garnett,
     Elizabeth

Nelson, Catherine 17

neo-classical style 8-9; and heraldry
     101

Nesfield, Henry Mills 25

Neville family, arms 30, 99

Newby Hall 46, 55, **65**, 66

Nollekens, Joseph, sculptor 8, 64, 67

Northcliffe, Faith and Fairfax 21

Norton family 10, 27; heraldry 96, 98, **98**

Norton, Mary 55

Norton, Sir Richard 32

obelisk in Ripon 54

Oriel College, Oxford, arms 104, **105**

Owen, Dean Charles Mansfield 41, **41**, 92; arms 104

Oxley family 9, **9**, 19, 40, 57-62; arms **108**

Oxley, Admiral Charles Lister 58

Oxley, Commander Christopher Bernard 62

parish registers 111-12, 114-15

Paul the Hermit, St 37

Peale, Charles Willson 69

Peckitt, William, glazier 10, 97

Peter, St 94

Pietà, sculpture 10, **10**

Pigott, arms 102, **102**, **103**

Pitt, William, Earl of Chatham 69

plague, 17th century 112, 113, 114

politicians 84

Porteous, Bishop Beilby 72, 83-4

Porteous, Robert 70, 72-4, **73**;

family tree **70**; arms 97

Price, Bishop Stuart Hetley 42-3

quartered arms **97**, **98**, **100**, **101**, **102**, **105**, **107**, 108, **108**

railway accident 22-3

Ramsden, Lt Col 58

Raper, Henry 15

Raynforth, Richard 114

recusancy 45

registers, parish 111-12, 114-5

reredos 9, **9**, 91-4, **92**, **93**, **94**

Ripley, Hugh, Wakeman 8, **8**, 50-1, **50**; arms 95-6, **96**

Ripley church 102

Ripon, Marquess of see Robinson, George Frederick

Ripon city, arms **98**, 104, **105**

Ripon city, 17th century map **47**

Ripon Diocese, arms 104, **104**

Ripon, St Wilfrid's Roman Catholic church 84

Rippon Hall, Virginia 68-9, **69**

Rippone Park 76

Rising of the North 32

Robinson, George Frederick, Marquess of Ripon 84, 98, **98**

Robinson, John, Bishop of London, arms **105**

Robinson, Thomas Philip, 3rd Baron

Grantham 67

Ross (Roos) family, arms 29, 30, 31, 99

Roundheads *see* Civil War

Royal arms 98, 103, **103**

Royal Artillery 90

sailors, memorials to 80-2

Sanderson, Lt Col Ronald Harcourt 90; arms **97**

Savage, Archbishop Thomas, arms 102, **102**

Scarborough Castle 45

Scrope arms 30

serpents 18-19, **18**, **19**, 65

singing-men, deaths 114

Skelton-on-Ure church 64

slavery, in America 72-3, 83-4

Slingsby arms 30

Smith, H.A.B.Bernard-, artist 92, **92**

Smith, William Slayter 78-9, **79**

Smithe, Ann (alias Ann Houghton), executed 113

snakes *see* serpents

Society of Dilettanti 64, 66

soldiers, memorials to 76-9

Soothill arms 29, 99, **99**

South Sea Company 52-4, 84

Stafford arms 30

Staveley family, arms **108**

Staveley, General Miles 76-7

Staveley, Robert Arthur Miles 77

Staveley, Simon **76**, 77

Stevenson, Isabella 21

Strickland, Henry William 6, 18, **18**, 25, **25**

Studley Royal 52, 54, **54**; garden 84

Studley Royal church 64, 84

Submarine C34 88, **89**

Sutton arms 30

Swales, arms 96, **97**

Sykes family 11

Sylph, HMS **80**, 81

symbols 18-19

Tasso, quoted 9, 40

Taylor, Anthony 48

Terry family 16

Terry, Anna and William 25

Thompson, Edward 73

Todd, arms 100, **100**

tombs, altar and table 116, **116**

tools, workmen's 19, **19**, **23**

Topcliffe church brass 36

Tunstall, Bryan 17

United States *see* America

Venus, Barberini 67

Vyner family, arms 98, **98**

Vyner, Frederick Grantham 63-4; arms **64**

Waddilove, Lt Francis William 77-8, 79

Waddilove, Dean Robert Darley 39, **39**, 58

Waddilove, Lt Robert James Darley, RN 18, **18**, **79**, 80-1

Wailes, William, glazier 10

Wakeman *see* Ripley, Hugh

Walbran, John Richard 30-1

Walker, Thomas and Mary 114

war memorials 86-93; reredos 91-4

Ward arms 29, 31, 102, **103**

Warlasse, Stephen 114

Washington, George and family 10, 69, 72; arms 71, **71**

Webber, Dean James, and family 9, **9**, 40-1, **40**

Weddell, Elizabeth 66

Weddell, William 8, **8**, 19, **19**, 64-7, **65**, **66**; arms 97, **97**, 101

Wentworth, arms 96, **97**

West Tanfield church 28

West Yorkshire Regiment 85, 88, 90, 91

Whitaker family 22; arms **107**

Whitaker, Fanny 22-3, **22**

Whitton, Robert, sculptor 82

Wilfrid, St, 94; attributed arms 104, **105**

window 11-12, **11**

Willement, Thomas, glazier 10, 96, 97, 98, **98**

William, St, of York, attributed arms 104, **105**

Williams, Canon John Gordon 43, **43**

Wilson, Henry, artist 9, 104

Wilson, John 14

Wilson, Thomas, sexton 117

Wilson, Warren 12

windows, heraldry in 96-8 *see also* glass

women, memorials to 20-6 use of arms by 107, 107-8, **107**

Wood, Henry Richard 101-2, **101**

wood, use in memorials 9, 10

Wooles, Paul 31

woollen, burial in 115

World War I memorials 86-91; reredos 91-4

Wyvil, Dean Christopher 20

York, Frederick, Duke of 77

York Diocese, arms **102**, 104, **105**

Yorke, Mary 55

Young, Bishop David 42

Epitaph for Ann, the wife of George Brigham,
died 8th May, 1791, aged 29:

Consider reader as you look

How suddenly this soul was took;

I pray take warning at its fall

And be ready at Christ's call.

Death does not always warning give,

Therefore, be cautious how you live,

And learn to die, for die you must,

And die to live amongst the just.

WILSON, T.: "*A verbatim copy of all the monuments, gravestones and other sepulchral memorials in Ripon Cathedral and its burial ground.*" (1847)

Facing page: the Norton window